THE REGICIDES

D1548592

also by A.L. Rowse:

Four Caroline Portraits
Reflections on the Puritan Revolution
Milton the Puritan: Portrait of a Mind
Jonathan Swift: Major Prophet

THE REGICIDES

and the Puritan Revolution

A.L. Rowse

Duckworth

DA
419.5
.A1
R69
1994

First published in 1994
Gerald Duckworth & Co. Ltd.
The Old Piano Factory
48 Hoxton Square, London N1 6PB
Tel: 071 729 5986
Fax: 071 729 0015

© 1994 by A.L. Rowse

All rights reserved. No part of this publication
may be reproduced, stored in a retrieval system, or
transmitted, in any form or by any means, electronic,
mechanical, photocopying, recording or otherwise
without the prior permission of the publisher.

A catalogue record for this book is available
from the British Library

ISBN 0 7156 2607 8

Picture credits

The author and publishers are grateful to the following for
supplying and giving permission to reproduce illustrations: Plate
1: The Royal Collection, © Her Majesty The Queen. Plates 2, 4, 5,
7, 8, 9, 10, 11: National Portrait Gallery. Plate 3: Fitzwilliam
Museum, University of Cambridge. Plate 6: The Lord Tollemache,
Helmingham Hall; photo: Courtauld Institute of Art. Plates 12, 13,
14: Ashmolean Museum, Oxford.

Photoset in North Wales by
Derek Doyle & Associates, Mold, Clwyd
Printed in Great Britain by
Redwood Books , Trowbridge

Contents

The history of the world is the
record of the weaknesses, frailty
and death of public opinions.

Samuel Butler

Plates

(between pages 64 and 65)

Preface

I am most grateful to my publisher, Colin Haycraft, for suggesting this subject – but for him I should not have thought of it – curiously enough, for it is an obvious sequel to my *Reflections on the Puritan Revolution*. Here is the tragic upshot to which Puritan propaganda and revolution led.

A reviewer of that earlier work, a second-rate professor, thought it a work of self-indulgence. In other words, a labour of love. For of course one should enjoy oneself in writing a book. Is it because professors do not enjoy writing their books that professorial works are apt to be dull? Today, in the discouraging conditions of the breakdown of standards of every kind – social and political, moral and artistic – they write for their own sub-culture, not for the general public.

Not so this book. 'If only the sense of *actuality* can be lulled,' writes E.M. Forster, 'and it sleeps for ever in most historians ...' I hope not here. I am not discouraged, for I am always passionately interested *in the subject in and for itself*, not in the views of people not up to the level of it.

Nor does it discourage me that, though the subject has salutary lessons, even morals to be drawn for the breakdown of society today (not only in the

Communist world), no heed will be taken. For me the subject is all in all – though I hope the attentive reader may gain not a few laughs from the distasteful subject.

A.L.R.

CHAPTER 1

Who Were the Regicides?

The Regicides were those people who sat in the so-called High Court of Justice that condemned Charles I to death in January 1649, along with a few others who did not sit but were fatally incriminated. 'Patricide' and 'matricide' – killing your father and mother – are ugly terms. But in the seventeenth century, when the king was thought of as Father of his country, the term 'regicide' – killing him – had a more dreadful import.

The killing of Charles I stunned the country and shocked Europe. In England it was said that one person died of the shock. It was totally against the wish and conscience of the country at large, and was never forgotten nor forgiven.

How then did this unprecedented and unforgivable event come about?

It was the work of the Army, or a section of it, in the Puritan Revolution after the Second Civil War. The First Civil War had finished with what was regarded as the complete victory of the Puritan Army – Naseby and all that.

But there remained the King. Early in the struggle a Parliamentarian had said, 'However many victories we win, there will still remain the King.' The monarch was indeed the linchpin of the constitutional structure, the pivot that held the fabric together. King, Lords and Commons formed the ancient, well-tried constitution, and few there were who could think of the country without its head.

The First Civil War had not resolved the issue – it was only a victory of force on the battlefield by the party stronger in arms. At any moment the country at large would have voted the King back, though the idea of 'voting' him is anachronistic: he was there by hereditary right, crowning the constitution.

Charles I was well aware of his rights, and knew that it was only a minority of his subjects who had defeated him. Even most of those did not conceive of dispensing with monarchy. Scotland – after all Charles I was their own, born there – did not fancy a régime imposed by English radicals. Charles proceeded to play off these divided parties and fractious elements against each other; that produced a Scottish invasion, and a series of coincident risings around the country showed how unsettled it was.

The Puritans over two or three generations had shown themselves masters of propaganda. From all their pulpits, fasts and orgies of prayer-meetings resounded reproaches, accusations, libels on the King. All this in the language of their Bible mania. Throughout the war their leading clerical propagandist, the well-paid Stephen Marshall, preached his famous sermon, 'Curse ye, Meroz', some sixty-seven times, with its message of pushing things to their conclusion.

Now an implacable spirit was whipped up in the

1. Who Were the Regicides?

Army, the King was alone responsible: 'the Man of Blood' – Biblical term – should be brought to account. After an orgy of three days of prayer at Windsor, the Army resolved 'to call Charles Stuart, that Man of Blood, to an account for that blood he hath shed and the mischief he had done to his utmost, against the Lord's cause and people'. Puritan semantics: 'the Lord's cause' always means their own. As Ludlow, a Fifth Monarchy fanatic, put it in their choice Bible language: 'Blood defileth the land, and the land cannot be cleansed of the blood that it shed therein, but by the blood of him that shed it.' They might be said to be, in the literal sense of the word, a bloody lot.

At the eleventh hour their prey nearly escaped them. From his imprisonment in the Isle of Wight Charles I came to terms with the Puritan Parliament – what remained in being of the institution, a minority in itself. It agreed, by the treaty of Newport, that the King's concessions were satisfactory, and formed the basis for settlement and peace, which the country longed for.

Not so the Army, or the leading spirits in it. Another Fifth Monarchy fanatic, Major-General Harrison, let the cat out of the bag: upon the conclusion of such a treaty 'we shall be commanded by King and Parliament to disband – the which if we do, we are unavoidably destroyed'. Self-interest always prevails. The Army took control, and retained control all through the Revolution, right up to the Restoration of the ancient constitution – King, Lords and Commons – in 1660. Power talks: politics are primarily about power.

Petitions now poured in from the City for a treaty with the King: the few lords who remained at Westminster prayed for it. Cromwell remained away in the North waiting on events. His son-in-law Ireton, the lawyer intellect behind him, shut himself up at Windsor penning a long Remonstrance to Parliament rehearsing all the King's crimes, constructing the case against him.

Parliament was not to be persuaded; the Army leaders decided on a purge (a term so familiar in our time, but then carried out less barbarically). The Commons were purged of their civilian majority: some 140 MPs were extruded, leaving only some 50 or 60 to carry out the Army's purpose. That is to say, the mere minority of a minority pushed forward by willpower, as in all revolutions, Jacobins or Communists.

At last Oliver Cromwell's mind was made up. He had emerged as the Army's most dynamic and publicised leader. An upper-class man, he was never a republican. It is fair to him to say that, like the statesman Pym, he favoured a parliamentary monarchy, a king governing on Parliament's terms. He had gone as far as possible to persuade Charles to accept this solution – which was unthinkable to the King.

Cromwell, watching events as usual, was determined not to let the lead slip out of his hands. Arguments were but 'fleshly reasonings'. 'Thinkest thou in thy heart that the glorious dispensations of God point to this ruining hypocritical agreement?' He meant his victories in the field, and was sure that Charles would not adhere to any 'hypocritical agreement'. 'Let us look unto providences, they hang so together, have been so constant, so clear, unclouded.' This meant nothing but success: nothing succeeds like success, and they had been justified by success all along. 'What think you of Providence disposing the hearts of so many of God's people this way? We trust the same Lord who hath framed our minds in our actings is with us in this also.' The die was cast, 'desiring only to fear our great God that we do nothing against His will'.

In the seventeenth century when people asserted God's will they almost always, as I have noted, meant their own. (Were they unaware of that? History is largely influenced by men's unawareness.)

The official head of the Army was Lord General Fairfax. As an aristocrat, he did not approve – there are indications as to that – and he held aloof from the proceedings. There has been much argument why. But surely to anyone of political judgment the answer is clear. His duty was above all to maintain the unity of the Army. If the Army were divided there would be renewal of war, possibly social breakdown and anarchy. He could not go against the determined will of his second-in-command, Cromwell, now backed by the Army crying for action.

Plans were hurriedly rushed forward to create a court of 'justice' to try the King. Not everyone realised even now that that meant his death. For, as Algernon Sidney, though a republican doctrinaire, pointed out – the King could not be tried by any such court, nor indeed could anybody else. It had no authority. To this Oliver Cromwell: 'I tell you we will cut off his head with the crown upon it.'

An ordinance constituting a tribunal of three

judges with a jury of 150 commissioners was presented to the rump of the Lords. It was unanimously rejected. The three eminent lawyers named, though Parliamentarians, refused to serve. A new ordinance created a court of 135 commissioners who were to act as both judge and jury. A second-rate lawyer, one Bradshaw, was drafted to preside over it, was hipped up to as much dignity as possible: the Lord President, provided with a scarlet robe, a guard, and a steel-rimmed hat to protect him from possible attentions of the populace. Nearly one half of the commissioners named refused to serve. The remnant, those who did, were the Regicides.

No point here in going into the famous scene of the 'trial' in Westminster Hall. It turned into a triumph for the grave solitary person of the King, who consistently refused to plead since the 'Court' had no authority. Charles had always had some impediment in his speech, but in this moment of truth he spoke out clear. 'It is not my case alone, it is the freedom and liberty of the people of England. Pretend what you will, I stand more for their liberties. For if power without law may make laws, I do not know what subject in England can be sure of his life, or anything that he calls his own.' This was the simple truth.

Several times Bradshaw interrupted to get the King to plead, so that the witnesses lined up against him might disseminate their propaganda. All to no avail: the King never moved from his position that the 'Court' had no authority, and represented mere force, not justice. When the Lord General Fairfax was named, a masked lady called out, 'He has more wit [intelligence] than to be here.' This was Fairfax's wife, and was taken to show what he thought of the proceedings. When Bradshaw came to state the charge of 'treason in the name of the people of England', another of the two masked ladies called out: 'Not half, not a quarter of the people of England! Oliver Cromwell is a traitor.'

Oliver Cromwell might have agreed but for 'God's' will. He is reported to have said, with his usual excited rhetoric, 'If any man had deliberately designed such a thing, he would be the greatest traitor in the world. But the Providence of God has cast it up on them.' This means nothing but the course of events.

In fact Cromwell took the lead in forcing events. Eleven years later, when the Regicides were brought to book, several of them pleaded that they had been under pressure from him and Ireton. Sir Richard Ingoldsby claimed that Cromwell held the pen while he signed the warrant. The conscience of one John Downes was touched by the King's words. 'Have we hearts of stone? Are we men?' He tried to get up to make a protest: 'If I die for it, I must do it.' Cromwell quelled him. 'What ails thee? Art thou mad? Canst thou not sit still and be quiet?' He struggled to his feet, 'Sir, no: I cannot be quiet.'

The Hall was crammed with soldiery, no risks taken. Any sign of disturbance or questioning was met by the cries they were encouraged, or paid, to make: 'Justice! Justice! Execution!' Several others among the commissioners claimed years later that they had risen to protest, and several of those named refused to sign. They remembered at the signing Cromwell and Henry Marten inking each other's faces. Cromwell, like the hysterical manic-depressive he was, was apt to indulge in horse-play at moments of crisis. The King maintained a regal dignity throughout, and his were the last words: 'I am not suffered for to speak: expect what justice other people will have.'

In the end some fifty-nine signed the death warrant. These were the Regicides. Three or four more were so closely involved, like Hugh Peters, as to be regarded as no less guilty. At the Restoration forty-one of these miscreants were alive to be dealt with. Fifteen escaped abroad: three of these safest to New England, the New Jerusalem where the godly welcomed them and gave them protection. Five got to Germany and Holland, whence one returned to get his come-uppance. Three of these were nabbed by Downing, the ambassador who put pressure on the States to extradite them. Sir George Downing, a rather nasty man by all accounts, had been Cromwell's agent in Scotland, and so had his passage to work. Only nine signers suffered the full ghastly penalties of treason, plus four non-signers who were held no less guilty. It is remarkable that so many were spared death, especially considering the reaction of the mob. When the Fifth Monarchist Harrison was drawn on his sledge through the streets – unrepentant and affirming that all had been done by God's will – spectators cried, 'Where is your Good Old Cause now?' This was much to the point. They might equally have asked where now was 'God's' will?

CHAPTER 2

Revolutionary Background: The Purge

It may be well to give some idea of the revolutionary background to the action in which the Regicides had involved themselves and for which they were brought to book some eleven or more years later, when caught out by events. The revolutionary turning point took place in December 1648 with the great Purge the Army leaders carried through against the large majority of their employers, the House of Commons – some 70 per cent against only 15 per cent revolutionaries plus 18 per cent who were prepared to go along with them, or at least did not openly oppose. Revolutions are made by determined, fanatical minorities. The vast majority, even of the politically active nation, were paralysed by the speed of the action, when not overawed, threatened, or actually imprisoned.

Today we are more familiar with the character and tactics of political purges, from those carried out by Hitler and Stalin. In old-fashioned history text-books we used to learn about 'Pride's Purge' as if it were a simple action carried out by a simple

Colonel hardly heard of before or after.

It was of course a vastly more important operation, against not only the Puritan Parliament but the City of London itself, covering several days and involving complex moves. Essentially, Westminster and the City were both occupied by the Army, hurriedly brought up from Windsor for the purpose. As the Leveller John Lilburne observed, the Army leaders were in 'haste to London to force and break up the Parliament'.

Their haste was due to the fact that – at last! – on 5 December Parliament, dominated as it was by Puritan civilians, had voted in favour of coming to terms with the King. They should have done it before – now they were too late. The Army had no intention of being excluded by King and Parliament coming together and sending it packing and unpaid – after all its service, and victories, on Parliament's behalf.

The brain behind these moves was that of the dour fanatic, Henry Ireton, Cromwell's son-in-law, and his group of convinced believers. If the King had been allowed to get to London, as he wished, he would have been received with acclamation: the King-in-Parliament would have prevailed, perhaps the King might even have won his game. Ireton and his fellows were determined to prevent that: it was 'high time', he wrote, 'considering how the members of Belial [members of Parliament!] flocked this day about the righteous' [himself and his clique].

The actual head of the Army was Lord General Fairfax, but he was no politician and gave no lead. His mind was concentrated on maintaining unity in the Army, and getting its pay out of Parliament. So the decision rested with the Lieutenant-General, Cromwell, who – like the politician he was – kept his options open, watching the course of events, till the last moment. He kept away in the North, but an indication of how his mind was moving may be gathered from his secretary's tell-tale remark: 'I verily think that God will break that great idol the Parliament' – what a contrast with the way the very name of Parliament had been idolised in 1640! He hoped that God, i.e. themselves, would break 'that old job-trot form of government of King, Lords and Commons', i.e. make for revolution.

These hopeful remarks did not necessarily represent Cromwell's unformulated views. However, a political revolution might abort social revolution, which Levellers and the Left-wing Radicals demanded. Ireton's clear thinking was well up to dealing with them – keep them talking while he settled the political issue, i.e. who was to be on top. Levellers could then be dealt with later – as they were. Lilburne was cheated of his expectations: no wonder he regarded Ireton as a 'Machiavellian'. Cromwell was equally conservative socially: as a man of the governing class he did not need to be told that one couldn't govern the country from the bottom upwards.

The final offer of the Army to the King was such that no king could possibly accept and retain kingship. On its rejection Cromwell's mind was made up, and that was decisive. The King was to be disposed of. The historian concludes, the Levellers were 'headed off – but the price was Charles I's head'.[1] Cromwell attempted to persuade his official

---

[1] D. Underdown, *Pride's Purge: Politics in the Puritan Revolution*, 193.

superior, Fairfax: 'I know God teaches you.' This meant simply that success was what counted – superiority in arms the evidence: in a word, merely force. Might *is* Right.

No doubt he thought that he was following – as others of the Regicides felt assured – 'the dictates of Providence'. Humans are not very self-aware – particularly in earlier centuries; but the instinct of self-preservation was at work, if obscurely: if Charles I had regained power, Cromwell could have been called to account.

Altogether it seems that 186 MPs were expelled, and some 45 imprisoned, for longer or shorter periods according to their danger as opponents of the take-over of power. We may use that meiosis to contrast its English humanity with Hitler's murderous Purge of opponents in June 1934, or Stalin's bogus state-trials with their criminal consequences, which took in so many Leftist ideologues in the 1930s. The Army's Purge in December 1648 killed no one but the King – followed by his cousin, the Duke of Hamilton (who had mis-advised him about Scotland). The Purge left only one-third of the House – the Rump. Even so, there was strong opposition among the Rumpers to the King's being brought to trial. Only those who had declared their Dissent from the vote of 5 December in favour of the Treaty with the King were allowed to sit.

This was no formal gesture on the part of an obscure Army Colonel, one Pride, as we learned from the textbooks. It was Revolution.

On the part of the people there was no reaction. 'From one end of London to the other there were no tears' for the MPs. People were fed up: what they wanted was Peace. They did not get it from the dynamism of the fanatics who drove forward to the King's trial – any more than the idealists of 1789 or 1917 got peace, or what was hoped for. To whip up support and inflame the crowd Hugh Peters was called in as usual. His Fast-day sermon was preached in the courtyard of Whitehall: the daft crowd 'were amazed at the wonderful things they heard from him and the great appearances they saw of God among the soldiery'.

The Rump declared that power resided among the people. This was humbug, of course: neither Oliver Cromwell nor Henry Ireton believed that. In Cromwell's case it was his religious nonsense, sometimes bordering on hysteria, that at times of crisis overpowered his governing-class political sense. This indeed gave him the capacity to compromise and so achieve leadership among conflicting factions. Hence his broader appeal, perhaps too his personal charisma.

We observe how many of the actors in the events of the Purge naturally reappear as Regicides. These were not the leading figures in the Parliamentary conflict which had conducted the Civil War against the King. They came on the whole from a lower social stratum, 'drawn from less impressive social groups'.[2] Even in the Civil War itself, as Baxter and Mrs Hutchinson observed separately, the nobility and greater gentry were generally for King and Church, except in Puritan East Anglia and the Home Counties. A Puritan preacher noted that the

[2] *Ibid.*, 189.

common people from 'blind Wales, and other dark corners of the land [e.g. the West Country] were for the King; but the more knowing are apt to contradict and question.'

Anybody can contradict and question, but can they do the job of governing? Events were to show that they could not – any more than in Revolutionary France or Russia. In seventeenth-century England they were forced back upon a governing class leader, Cromwell, backed always by the Army, to fill the gap – in historical perspective, a hiatus.

Sir Robert Harley described his own Royalist Herefordshire as 'the most clownish county in England'. This Puritan was the enlightened spirit who presided over the destruction of the glorious stained glass in Henry VII's Chapel in Westminster Abbey and much else in the London churches.

Parliament's support had come mainly from the lesser gentry, the towns, especially London and the seaports, commercial and industrial sectors, particularly the clothing areas. Even Lord Burghley in his time had noticed that cloth-workers were less willing 'to be quietly governed than the husbandmen' – trade unionists in embryo, we might say.

Then there were the Puritan clergy, of whom a Commonwealth journalist said that 'every prayer is a stratagem, most sermons mere plots against the state'. Poor Charles I had ground for complaint: 'if the pulpits teach not obedience', how can the country be governed? In fact, Puritan pulpits preached *dis*-obedience: Parliamentarian Selden perceived that as clearly as authoritarian Hobbes. Popular preachers like Stephen Marshall and

2. Revolutionary Background: The Purge

Cornelius Burgess were trouble-makers, while Hugh Peters was a rabble-rouser. They were riddled with envy of the bishops, deans and higher clergy, inveighing against pluralities, and seizing the opportunity to get into them when the chance came – as the idealist Milton observed with disgust, fed up with triumphing Presbyterians. (But what could he expect of ordinary humans?)

In short, Parliament had had with it all the sort of people who envied those above them. Envy is a most powerful factor in human affairs, i.e. in history; it is odd that academics do not observe its operation, though themselves so much subject to it. It is particularly to the fore in all revolutions; we may regard it as a psychological precipitant.

The class situation at the back of the Civil War was then reflected in the High Court constituted to try the King, which was the aim and purpose of the Purge. Less than half of those whom the revolutionaries hoped to recruit to it consented to serve: 'on the whole it was the men of solidly established rank and status who drew back.'[3] Only one member of the peerage, the fanatic Lord Grey of Groby, took part in the proceedings of the court.

Of those peers who went along with the Revolution it was said at the time that Pembroke did so to save Wilton – if so, very sensible of him. Think of the destruction that overwhelmed the Marquis of Winchester's palace at Basing, Worcester's Raglan, Derby's Lathom, etc. The Cecil Earl of Salisbury, encisted in Parliamentarian Hertfordshire, sensibly

[3] *Ibid.*, 187.

saved Hatfield. Lord Lisle similarly ensured Penshurst. (His descendant said to me, 'Politics is about power – and Charles I had lost it.') Algernon Sidney of that family, though a doctrinaire republican, repudiated the court. Those two splendid Elizabethan palaces which had come to the Crown by purchase or exchange – Sir Christopher Hatton's Holdenby and Burghley's Theobalds – had gone to rack and ruin in the War, as had Henry VIII's fantasy palace of Nonsuch. All grievous losses. The Rumpers actually proposed the destruction of the English cathedrals as useless, the brutes. (It is always easier to replace such persons than masterpieces of art and architecture.)

Deans and canons of cathedrals were good for nothing but 'eating and drinking and getting up to piss'. This was an expressive Puritan view.

Of the eleven baronets called upon by the Rump's ordinance, only four responded. Among baronets who absented themselves two stand out. Sir William Brereton had very ably subdued Cheshire and the North West for Parliament, and was the king-pin there. Sir Arthur Hazelrig swayed the North East from Auckland Castle, which he had gobbled up from the bishopric of Durham. This Presbyterian pomposity had done well out of the war, and was notable for the ostentation of his carriages, velvet-dressed lackeys, etc. True, he was not notable for courage, having run away from Cheriton Field. Above all a politician, he now stayed away from the court. It could not be concluded, it has been well said, that the court 'represented the gentlemen of England'.

All the leading Parliamentary lawyers refused to

have anything to do with it, rejecting its legality. (Royalist lawyers of course were non-persons, or in exile, like Clarendon.) At the expulsion of the majority of MPs from Westminster the grotesque lawyer Prynne provided a comic touch. He got entangled in his long, old-fashioned sword, nearly tripped up, and was escorted out still arguing, protesting, gesticulating. He was always good for a joke, if he had not been so venomous, for it was he who drove poor Archbishop Laud to death.

It was notable that the conduct of the soldiery towards their betters during the Purge was civil and courteous – so different from a Continental Purge, German, Russian, or even French. Still, the Secluded were secluded, many imprisoned, the great body sent off into the wilderness for the next eleven years. For example, the impecunious Lord Say and Sele, whose prime motive had been to get his snout into the trough as Lord Treasurer (missing it, he had got a handsome compensation), now retreated to the fastness of Lundy Island. The rich and religious Lord Robartes, who had dominated the Parliamentarian cause in Cornwall, now retired to plant avenues at Lanhydrock – to return at the Restoration to pomp and glory, with a step-up in the peerage.

It might be said that the alliance between respectable Parliamentarians and Royalists that brought about the Restoration represented the aim of the Treaty of Newport, which the Purge had prevented. Charles I's son was restored, as his father had foreseen he would be – actually doing better than the Treaty provided, for he was restored virtually without conditions. In that sense, Charles I won the game by his victimisation and martyrdom.

CHAPTER 3

Cromwell and his Relations

Oliver Cromwell might well be called the Grand Regicide, for there is little doubt that, if it had not been for him, there would have been no 'trial' and execution of the King. He was an extraordinary phenomenon; we cannot go into his extraordinary career but merely regard him in relation to this central event.

Nor need there be any doubt that he was a great man, for he rose to greatness with every challenge which historic events presented to him. A.J.P. Taylor once said to me, 'When you say "a great man", you only mean that he is quicker on the trigger.' To this superficial, cheap cynicism, I replied: 'I have no bias in favour of Cromwell, but consider – (a) a civilian at the beginning of the war, by the end he proved himself the ablest commander in the field; (b) when the country was falling to pieces, with wars in all three kingdoms, he grasped the power to keep things together and proved the ability to exercise it. Surely this showed he was a great man.'

Clarendon, his great opponent, recognised it and paid tribute to Cromwell's 'greatness of heart' – meaning the largeness of capacity with which he

31

could conduct the affairs of three kingdoms and the patriotism that cared for their interest as one. Of Charles I Cromwell said that he was 'the hardest-hearted man on earth'. What this meant was that, underneath all Charles's shifts and evasions, there was stony ground. He was adamant about his royal prerogatives, and there nothing could move him. There is a certain truth in the traditional folklore of Cromwell's sighing 'Cruel Necessity', for he was a very human man, if not always humane, and there was something inhuman about the humanist Charles I.

Oliver Cromwell was both uncompromising when he reached a decision, and pragmatic in reaching it, opportunist as a politician must be. At the passing of the Grand Remonstrance by the Long Parliament, the then unknown member said that, if it had not passed, he would have sold all that he had and gone to America. Clarendon commented on this with his own sly humour, 'So near was this poor country to its deliverance.'

Cromwell was – as President Nixon said to this author about Eisenhower – 'always the politician'. Professor Trevor-Roper regarded Cromwell as a failure politically in dealing with his Parliaments. This is a misjudgment: there never was any hope of squaring the circle. Cromwell longed for power to rest on a constitutional basis; but the power of the Puritan Revolution rested on the basis of force, its Army. Cromwell could never dispense with that, and could never achieve a consensus. To speak anachronistically, a free vote at any time, had such a thing been possible, would have returned a king, Charles or his son. Cromwell, a supremely practical man in a world of religious lunatics and political doctrinaires, governed in accordance with the practical facts and exigencies of his situation. He could not get out of them.

He was a bit of a religious lunatic himself, but again made the utmost practical use of that. He talked, as he thought, in the language of the Bible mania of the time. This has always made unbelievers, and cultivated persons generally, regard him as a hypocrite. We must be more precise in our language, and more fair in judgment. Hypocrisy would mean that he, and those who talked this nauseating language – Puritan preachers intoned nasally, as in New England today – did not believe the nonsense they gave vent to. But they did, practically all of them. It would therefore be more exact to describe them not as hypocrites but as humbugs. It is comic to think that they humbugged themselves, and each other, a good deal. Cavalier commentators, newspapers and satirists, poets like Samuel Butler, popular street rhymes, got many a good laugh at them.

Oliver Cromwell, as an upper-class man, was socially conservative, no revolutionary. He described himself, modestly, as belonging to the middling gentry. But in fact the Cromwells went back to Henry VIII's great minister, who ended as Earl of Essex, and were solidly based on monastic lands. Oliver belonged to a cadet branch of the family, but his uncle turned the Benedictine monastery of Hinchinbrook into a mansion, where he lived in aristocratic style and entertained James I three times. Oliver himself married a Bourchier, of that medieval family, and with money.

He belonged to a widespread and powerful cousinage which included the rich St Johns, Wallers and Hampdens. John Hampden – that great 'trumpet of sedition' who became a cult-idol for raising hell among the gentry against Ship Money – was Cromwell's first cousin. Ship Money had been charged on coastal counties to raise money for ships for their defence. Why should it not be extended to inland counties which also enjoyed the defence the Navy provided for the whole country? Such was the argument of the King's Attorney-General Noy, a coastal Cornishman. The charge was minimal, John Hampden a very rich man. Clarendon tells us what magic his name had with the populace: we should say in the demotic language of today – a rabble-rouser.

The pure intellect behind Oliver Cromwell's hesitations and waitings and watchings was that of **Henry Ireton**, who became his son-in-law and had more influence than anyone on the great man up to the King's 'trial' and thereafter. Ireton was born in Nottinghamshire in 1611, the eldest son of well-to-do landed parents, both fervent Puritans. As a youth at Trinity College, Oxford, he was thought to be 'a stubborn and saucy fellow towards the seniors, and therefore his company was not at all wanting', i.e. wanted. He seems never to have been a popular type: an intellectual.

After a spell at Middle Temple which made him a lawyer, he returned to his estate in Notts, where his fellow country woman, Mrs Hutchinson, said of him, 'Having had an education in the strictest way of godliness, and being a man of good learning, great understanding and other abilities, he was the chief promoter of the Parliament's interest in the county.' Supercilious, self-righteous Lucy Hutchinson did not approve of many people: Henry Ireton could not be faulted.

He was a man of a clear determination who seems not to have had any doubts. Strait-laced Presbyterians thought him 'a mere Anabaptist' – this merely meant that he was Independent-minded. Courageously he fought his way all through the civil war. He was very critical of his commander, the half-hearted Earl of Manchester, who was the man who thought that however often they beat the King he still remained king. As ready with his pen as with the sword, Ireton wrote in a damaging deposition against the Earl, in support of Cromwell's campaign to get him out. Cromwell's position was – Why take up arms if you are not going to push them home to final victory? (All very well, but then what?)

Out of this conflict came the New Model Army that won the war, and Ireton achieved increasingly close contact with Cromwell through all the confusion that emerged from that. Often Cromwell, whose sympathies were much wider, kept his ear to the ground, listened to his inner voice, and had his doubts. The young man helped to clear up his mind for him. In return the experience of the older man often moderated the sharpness and narrowness of youth.

Ireton was wounded and taken prisoner at Naseby but escaped by a clever ruse. Increasingly at hand in negotiations, he was engaged in those for the surrender of Oxford, where he engaged himself to Oliver's daughter Bridget. They were married a few days before the surrender, at a private mansion on the hill at Holton overlooking the city. The bridegroom was already thirty-four.

Political confusion and social discontent spread on every hand. Most dangerous were the demands of the soldiery for arrears of pay, and not only for pay but for a say in the disposition of things which they had won for their betters. The irrepressible John Lilburne gave voice to Leveller demands spreading in the Army, for votes, for better representation in Parliament, more frequent Parliaments. This was anathema to the stiff-necked Presbyterians who dominated the House: they were oligarchs, who wanted to take the King's place in power, but not to share it with the lower classes.

Lilburne, 'Honest John', belonged to a North Country family which was doing well out of confiscated Royalist lands, and brother Robert was a Regicide. Cromwell was very patient with this trouble-maker: needs must, as a good politician. He employed Ireton's pen to argue the case put forward by Lilburne's incessant pamphleteering. Ireton argued back that the demand for universal suffrage was destructive of property, the foundation of society, and no less of liberty at large. He meant the liberty of those people who had a 'stake' in the country. 'He detested the abstract theories of Natural Right on which the Levellers based their demands.'

As the crisis grew, and was yet unresolved, it was necessary to make concessions to the Left, or at least to appear to do so. Ireton now took a line 'in such wise both for matter and manner as we believe will not only refresh the bowels of the Saints, but be of satisfaction to every honest member of Parliament'. 'Honest' meant those who agreed with him and the Army. But the great majority of the Saints in Parliament did not, so Ireton took a leading part in making out the list for Colonel Pride to extrude them.

The Levellers needed to be lulled along until the King was dealt with. Now Ireton was prepared to use their appeal to Natural Law for that purpose, since there was no better authority for it, indeed none at all. In his *Remonstrance of the Army* to Parliament 'the doctrine of the sovereignty of the people is employed throughout'. He argued naughtily that anyway the Army was as representative of the people as *they* were – a lawyer's *argumentum ad homines*, but hard to refute. As for Natural Law – well, it 'had to be employed in situations where precedents were lacking'. Of course.

The charge against the King at his 'trial' was essentially based upon the case Ireton made out. We are told that 'the *Remonstrance*'s most important function was to provide the ideological justification for the extra-legal actions – the purging of Parliament, and the "trial" and execution of the King'. Justification! Who was taken in by it? It was the naked use of power, as the King said. Politics = power; power = politics. Political theorising is largely a defence for one's own interests. We need waste no time over ideological justification any more than 'God's will'.

We are told that Ireton's Leftist *Remonstrance* had 'the effect of keeping the Levellers distracted while the Army officers carried out their version of a revolution – execution of a king, without social transformation'. The Levellers 'were easily squashed, with General Ireton actively engaged in the process. No wonder Lilburne regarded Ireton as "the cunningest of Machiavellians".'

This is an unfair judgment. Ireton was a practical man. In seventeenth-century circumstances the idea of universal suffrage was ludicrous; even today, three centuries later, in all the enlightenment of our time, it does not yield unadulterated satisfaction. Even if we were to take their nostrums seriously, we might accept that a little fairer representation of localities makes sense, but fresh Parliaments every two years? Simply silly.

We need go no further into Ireton's strenuous, overworked short life. When Cromwell set out to subjugate Ireland, and answer the Massacre of Protestants by expulsion of Catholics to beyond the Shannon, Ireton went as his second-in-command, and succeeded him as Deputy. He took no thought for appearances or care of his bodily health: he worked himself to death, dying of fever there when just forty. Within a year Bridget Cromwell married his successor, General Fleetwood.

Ireton was given a magnificent funeral in Westminster Abbey – good propaganda. This would have been contrary to his strict tastes. When offered £2000 by Parliament in reward for his services, he rejected it. (Not so Cromwell: He accepted everything that was the Lord's will.)

At the Restoration all this was unscrambled (was that the Lord's will too?) Their coffins were taken up, along with Bradshaw's, their bodies hung in chains on the gallows at Tyburn, then buried beneath.

3. Cromwell and his Relations

Of the tributes to this remarkable man his fellow Regicide, Hewson, wrote: 'We know no man like-minded, most seeking their own things, few so singly minded the things of Jesus Christ, of the interest of the precious sons of Zion.' Clarendon described him less ecstatically but more revealingly, as was his wont: 'a man of a melancholic, reserved, dark nature, who communicated his thoughts to very few, so that for the most part he resolved alone. He was thought often by his obstinacy to prevail over Cromwell, but that proceeded only from his dissembling less; for he was never reserved in the communicating his worst and most barbarous purposes, which the other always concealed and disavowed.'

This is unfair to Cromwell, it only means that he was the better politician.

When one looks at Ireton's portrait it is the face of a lean, mean, hungry-looking intellectual, a severe Puritan. A Royalist newspaper pretended a hue-and-cry after him: 'A tall black thief, with bushy curled hair; a meager, envious face, sunk hollow eyes; a complexion between choler and melancholy, a four-square Machiavellian head, and a nose of the fifteens.'

No joke is recorded of him – and indeed he was no joke.

Valentine Walton (one did not pronounce the *l* in those days, so he usually appears as Waughton) was Cromwell's brother-in-law, having married his sister Margaret. He too belonged to the landed gentry (Great Staughton) of the horribly Puritan county of Huntingdon. An ancestor had been

Speaker of the House of Commons in the 15th century, so his election to represent his county in the Long Parliament in 1640 was appropriate. His next appearance on the scene of public affairs was when he helped his brother-in-law's decisive pounce on the plate of the Cambridge colleges, stopping it from being sent to the King's aid. On the whole they were as loyal as those at Oxford, most of which gave up all their medieval plate (hence All Souls, for instance, has none left).

Walton raised a troop of horse which served at Edgehill, where he was taken prisoner. Exchanged next year for a Royalist equivalent he became colonel of a regiment in the irreducible Eastern Association. At the ghastly battle of Marston Moor, which claimed fearful casualties in the summer of 1644, his son was mortally wounded. Cromwell wrote, 'from the leaguer before York, To my loving brother, Colonel Valentine Walton, These':

> It's our duty to sympathise in all mercies, and to praise the Lord together in all chastisements or trials, that so we may sorrow together. Truly England and the Church of God hath had a great favour from the Lord, in this great Victory given unto us. It had all the evidences of an absolute Victory obtained by the Lord's blessing upon the Godly Party principally ... God made them as stubble to our swords. I believe, of Twenty thousand the Prince [Rupert] hath not Four thousand left. Give glory, all the glory, to God.

Though the language is sickening, the numbers as

usual are probably exaggerated. Then:

> Sir, God hath taken away your eldest Son by a
> cannon shot. It brake his leg. We were
> necessitated to have it cut off, whereof he died.
> But the Lord took him into the happiness we all
> pant for and live for. There is your precious
> child full of glory, never to know sin or sorrow
> any more. He was a gallant young man,
> exceedingly gracious.
>
> One thing lay upon his spirit. He told me it
> was, That God had not suffered him to be any
> more the executioner of His enemies.

Such was the spirit of the fierce New Model Army.
His uncle continues:

> I am told he bid them, Open to the right and left
> that he might see the rogues run. Truly he was
> exceedingly beloved in the Army, of all that
> knew him. But few knew him, for he was a
> precious young man, fit for God. You have cause
> to bless the Lord. He is a glorious Saint in
> Heaven: wherein you ought exceedingly to
> rejoice. Let this public mercy to the Church of
> God make you to forget your private sorrow.

It is all nauseating, but such is the language the
Saints talked, Oliver Cromwell being especially
given to it.

The Puritan victory at Marston Moor, with its
great slaughter, was only partially offset by the
King's victory in Cornwall and the surrender of
Essex's army, by which fewer lives were lost.
Cromwell wrote again:

We do with grief of heart resent the sad condition of our Army in the West, and of affairs there.

Was this also the Lord's doing?

Indeed we never find our men so cheerful as when there is work to do. The Lord is our strength, and in Him is all our hope. Pray for us.

I write but seldom: it gives me a little ease to pour my mind, in the midst of calumnies, into the bosom of a Friend.

These calumnies were to the effect that 'we seek to maintain our opinions in religion by force ...' What a shocking aspersion! 'I profess I could never satisfy myself of the justness of this War, but from the Authority of the Parliament to maintain itself in its rights. And in this Cause I hope to approve myself an honest man.'

Within a few years he was to put his foot through Parliament and send it packing. The move was popular: the People of England, who had been so mad for Parliament beforehand – witness Clarendon – just didn't care any more. But this was what made true believers in the Good Old Cause, when Oliver made himself Lord Protector and would have been king, think him a dishonest man. Himself didn't think so. Naturally not.

As governor of King's Lynn, Walton heavily fortified it. The Presbyterians in Parliament said, in their friendly way, that he prepared it as a refuge in case his party, the Independents, should need it.

3. Cromwell and his Relations

From Lynn, in May 1646, he was able to report to Parliament – with his fellow Regicide-to-be, Miles Corbet – on the wanderings of the King from Oxford in disguise on his way to betrayal by his fellow Scots (they sold him to Parliament for a large sum):

It doth appear to us that Mr Hudson, the parson that came from Oxford with the King, was at Downham in Norfolk with two other gentlemen. The 2 of May they came to a blind alehouse at Crimplesham, about 8 miles from Lynn. From thence Mr Hudson did ride to Downham again ... Hudson was then in a scarlet coat. There he met with Mr Ralph Skipwith of his former acquaintance, and with him he did exchange his horse ... Hudson procured the said Skipwith to get a grey coat for the Dr (as he called the King). The King put off his black coat and long cassock, and put on Mr Skipwith's grey coat. The King bought a new hat at Downham, and went into the Isle of Ely. Wherever they came they were very private, and always writing. Hudson did inquire for a ship to go to the North, or Newcastle, but could get none.

And so the poor King passed on his *via dolorosa*, attended by the chaplain from Queen's College and the faithful John Ashburnham. At Ashburnham's home I have seen in my time the shirt the King wore on the scaffold, faint blood-stains still visible. Up to last century it was still touched by the faithful, for the King's Evil.

Walton had no trouble of conscience in signing the King's death warrant; but, a sincere republican, did have over his brother-in-law becoming Protector. At Oliver Cromwell's death he reappeared with the Rump, and was given command of Desborough's regiment (Cromwell's cousin). At the Restoration he lost the considerable estates he had purchased, from what had been the Queen's dowry. Exempt from the Act of Oblivion, he sensibly fled abroad to Hanau, where fellow Protestants gave him a welcome and made him a townsman. There he died, in such obscurity no one knows when.

Edward Whalley was a cousin of Cromwell's. Along with Ireton and Hutchinson he made a third Regicide from Notts, a bad lot for the county. A younger son of small gentry, he was apprenticed to a woollen draper in the City, and like any young man joined up with alacrity at the beginning of the War, ready to fight. Would a duck swim? He made a good fighting man. Early on, at Gainsborough, in Cromwell's regiment of horse, he distinguished himself. Cromwell wrote, 'the honour of this retreat is due to God, as also all the rest. Major Whalley did in this carry himself with all gallantry becoming a gentleman and a Christian.'

He was no fanatic. Baxter, the garrulous chaplain of his regiment, said that he was superseded as colonel because he did not favour the sectaries and thus was not in favour at headquarters. He was orthodox enough, but perhaps not very religious. He was better at fighting, and had a good record as such in the War: at Naseby, the storming of Bristol; the surrender of Oxford, Banbury, Worcester. He identified himself with his men, represented their grievances to Parliament, and took a leading part in opposing their disbandment.

When the King was confined at Holdenby, Parliament inflicted upon him a bevy of Puritan humbugs who held up meals with their intolerable prayers and long graces. The King took no notice of them, said a brief grace for himself and went on with his meal. When he was shifted to Hampton Court, Whalley was placed in charge and treated the King with civility and courtesy. He refused to accept Parliament's infliction of Puritan humbugs upon him – the King was attended by civilised Anglican chaplains.

Parliament was determined that the King should not come to London, as he asked, where there would be demonstrations in his favour and a reaction set in. Otherwise, Whalley allowed fairly free access, and Charles received many visitors. Particularly the Scottish commissioners with whom he was negotiating, getting them to intervene. Naturally enough – but it laid the ground for the Second Civil War.

Cromwell wrote a letter warning of danger to the King's life, and certainly he feared assassination. But what was the intention of the letter? Where Oliver Cromwell was concerned people often could not be sure. With his ear to the ground he must have known of the Scottish emissaries. Did he intend to alarm Charles, flush the bird from his nest?

That certainly was its effect. It precipitated Charles's fatal flight to the Isle of Wight, where he could be held in absolute security to await the Army's decision.

We have a long report from Whalley to Speaker Lenthall detailing the King's days at Hampton Court and his flight. He was not kept by Whalley as a prisoner, but gave him word that he would not depart without some warning. His children came to stay with him three or four days. His eldest daughter, Princess Elizabeth was lodged in a room opening out from the long gallery. She complained of the tramp of the soldiers going up and down; Whalley did his best to quieten them.

He showed Cromwell's letter to the King, since 'the letter indicates some murderous design, or at least some fear of it, against his Majesty'. Whalley wished to assure him that, though there were frequent menaces against him, 'our general officers abhorred so bloody and villainous a fact'. Charles gave the Colonel some indication that he might make for another of his houses, and, when he vanished, he left a letter of thanks to him for his courteous behaviour.

Whalley took his place along with the rest in the High Court of Justice and signed up, but took no part in politics. He remained the soldier, fighting prominently at Dunbar, where he was wounded and had his horse killed under him, as often happened.

There was an appalling slaughter of horses – one's heart goes out to the poor creatures – in the human idiocy of these wars. So great that, later in the century, there had to be a large import of Arab horses – the Godolphin Arabian and such – to renew the best bloodstock.

At the Restoration Whalley lost the considerable estates he had built up when the going was good. He had bought a manor of the Royalist Marquis of Newcastle's, two more of the Queen's lands, while Parliament had awarded him lands worth £500 a year in Scotland for his services there.

Since he was excepted from the Act of Indemnity and Oblivion – Indemnity for the King's enemies and Oblivion for his friends, said impoverished Royalists, who got nothing back – Whalley skipped overseas, with his son-in-law Major-General Goff and the obscure John Dixwell. All were liable to the extreme penalties of the law.

They were lucky in making for the heavenly Jerusalem of Boston, 'a city set as it were upon an hill', to be a light to lighten the Gentiles. There they were protected by the godly. Agents were sent in pursuit of them, so they were moved about from place to place, to Hadley, to Newhaven. I remember to have been shown a cave in the latter vicinity, where one or the other of them was supposed to have lurked. As time went on they could creep out of their holes and corners in some security.

Whalley survived until at least 1674, for a letter from his son-in-law described him then as 'scarce capable of any rational discourse, his understanding, memory and speech doth so much fail him, and seems not to take much notice of anything that is either done or said, but patiently bears all things'.

He had had a very wearing life. Perhaps he had come to realise at last that of 'anything that is either done or said', especially in politics, it is not worth taking 'much notice'. We learn that John Davenport, a founder of New England, personally sheltered the miscreants, and 'had no compunction in dissembling to the king's agents'. Of course not: were they not all Saints?

Yet Archbishop Laud had written kindly of Davenport, 'a most religious man who fled to New England for the sake of a good conscience'. Puritans would never write kindly of the poor Archbishop, for whom they had nothing but venom and lies, eventually pursuing him to death.

Sir Richard Ingoldsby was another of Cromwell's blooming cousinage. He was just a soldier, no politician, and it is a relief to learn that he 'could neither pray nor preach'. Cromwell's ascendancy was due to his being both, supreme as soldier *and* politician, and histrionically, as well as hysterically, religious in a time of religious mania. He could certainly both pray and preach. Ingoldsby, no fanatic, kept to his cousin's coat-tails throughout the whole *épopée*.

The second son of a Buckinghamshire knight, his mother was the daughter of the grand Hinchinbrook Cromwells. He began as a young captain in his cousin Hampden's regiment, then went on to be a colonel in Cromwell's New Model Army. He took part in the storming of Bristol and Bridgwater, and in the reduction of the Royalist West.

His regiment, which was garrisoning Oxford, refused to be disbanded even when Parliament sent them their pay. They petitioned against any treaty with the King and demanded his punishment. Ingoldsby complied, but did not attend any of the sessions of the High Court. He pleaded later that his signature to the death warrant had been extorted from him by his implacable cousin, who put 'the pen between his fingers, with his own hand writ *Richard Ingoldsby*, he making all the resistance he could'.

This may or may not be true – one would not put it past *that* cousin.

Ingoldsby continued to have trouble from the

Levellers in his regiment at Oxford, who made New College their headquarters (it should have been Balliol). They shut him up in one of the inns, from which his captain got him out. Together they easily gave the rank-and-file their come-uppance.

With upper-class realism Ingoldsby saw when, with Oliver Cromwell's death, the régime was breaking down, and began to work his passage with the King abroad. He approached the Earl of Northampton to declare to Charles II that 'your pardon and forgiveness of his former errors was all that he aimed at'.

He made common cause with Monk, who always had been a Royalist, and served that cause by suppressing Lambert's rebellion – a forlorn hope, for his men would not fight for him. Ingoldsby sought no reward, but at the Restoration he got one. At the coronation, which was exceptionally grand and ceremonious, to mark that the lugubrious days of the Saints were over, Ingoldsby was made a Knight of the Bath according to the old tradition.

He married the widow of a Lee of Hartwell, and was buried in that beautiful church, ruined in our own lugubrious time.

Simon Mayne was Cromwell's cousin by marriage, and otherwise related to several Regicides. Henry Marten was his mother's brother-in-law; Robert Lilburne his niece's husband; James Temple another cousin. What a crew! I suppose they confabulated together. Mayne certainly did with Thomas Scott, fellow-Regicide and also MP for Aylesbury, for those two controlled the affairs of Buckinghamshire. Mayne was rich and grasping: he inherited considerable estates, with the fine mansion of Dinton Hall, the historic house that still survives, but wanted more. He got sequestered estates belonging to the Dean and Chapter of Rochester, through Henry Marten as mediary, who was not interested in property (he wasted away his own) but in women.

Mayne ran his County Committee with a high hand, refusing to submit his accounts to Parliament for moneys received from sequestered Royalist estates. When asked for them he replied that their ordinance had given him complete authority to do as he thought fit. He said that the money had been spent on raising a troop of militia horse and paying Bucks soldiers. He then added curtly that *his* troops had been properly paid, 'not necessitated to wait at the Parliament's doors with petitions for the same' as with many other counties. Parliament did not reply that other counties submitted their accounts properly and obediently.

He attended the High Court regularly, along with the three other Bucks renegades, Challoner, Fleetwood and Scott. Mayne claimed that Challoner had made him sign the death warrant and boasted that he was the one who had 'made Mr Mayne a man of courage and resolution'. Maybe – who knows the truth?

Anyway he was not executed. Not yet fifty he died next year in the Tower. His son recovered his estates, and the family went on at Dinton. Why was the Restoration government so reasonable and accommodating? – Clearly they did not want to upset the social structure any further.

3. Cromwell and his Relations

Richard Deane was related, through his mother, to John Hampden and Cromwell, as well as to other Puritan worthies. He was a professional soldier, a gunner, in charge of the artillery at Naseby. Thus Cromwell made him Comptroller of Ordnance. He took a leading rôle in crushing the various revolts which largely made up the Second Civil War, and in defeating the Scots – who had gone back on their hostility to Charles I – at Preston. He was an active co-operator in bringing Charles to account, helping to fix time and place for his execution.

That year he was appointed one of the Generals at Sea, since naval commands were still given to soldiers, as in Elizabethan days. He conveyed Cromwell's expedition to Ireland, and joined in the land fighting. He also commanded the fleet that supported Cromwell's campaign in Scotland.

In the Commonwealth's war on Holland Deane was killed by the first Dutch broadside, as he stood on the deck of his flagship, with the Puritan name, *Resolution*. (It might as well have been 'Revolution'.) Cromwell ordered a public funeral, and administered his usual grave consolation to the widow personally.

Deane was buried in Henry VII's chapel, disinterred at the Restoration, but given respectful burial in a neighbouring churchyard. For he was regarded as a national hero, like Robert Blake – and as Cromwell might have been but for his crime.

John Jones was already well on in his career when he married, as his second wife, Cromwell's sister, Catherine. He was Welsh, from North Wales, while Cromwell had a Welsh streak through his Williams ancestry. Jones made his name by subduing the Royalist stronghold of Anglesey, whence the Tudors had come.

He was next in the front line in Ireland, an inextricable maze. The Papal nuncio, Rinuccini, wanted to reduce the country to a Papal fiefdom, and was bad at co-operating with native Irish. The Royalist leader, Ormonde, was opposed by the purer Protestants. In the North were the Scotch Presbyterians. No decision, until Cromwell descended like a thunderbolt on the distracted country.

Jones was an able commander. His fellow Regicide Ludlow paid tribute to his 'diligence, ability, and integrity in providing for the happiness of that country [no one could!], and bringing to justice those who have been concerned in the murders of the English Protestants'.

Jones's republicanism put him against the Cromwells' monarchical pretensions. Henry Cromwell reported him as 'endeavouring to render the government unacceptable, but more cunning and close' in his opposition than Ludlow. Then Jones married the Protector's sister. Thereupon Henry to Thurloe: 'When I writ to you about Colonel Jones, I did not know that he was likely to be my uncle. Perhaps that may serve to oblige him to faithfulness to his Highness [Oliver would have preferred it to be his Majesty] and government.' Someone else wrote that 'he might have been a great man indeed, did not something stick which he cannot well get down. He is not thorough-paced for the Court proceedings, nor is his conscience fully hardened against the Good Old Cause.'

That was what stuck in his gullet – his republican

conscience. At the Restoration he made no attempt to fly, to sue for pardon, or repent. He was walking quietly in Finsbury when he was arrested and sent to the Tower. No mercy for him. At his execution he conducted himself with dignity and soldierly courage. Cromwell would have been proud of his brother-in-law.

When Mr Pepys heard, in December 1660, that the bodies of the leading Regicides were to be thrown out of the Abbey and hanged at Tyburn, he was rather sorry for the fate of the Grand Regicide: 'which, methinks, do trouble me that a man of so great courage, as he was, should have that dishonour – though otherwise he might deserve it enough.'

CHAPTER 4

Fifth Monarchy Fanatics

Recent commemoration of the English Translation of the Bible concentrated on the nobility of its language, and the widespread influence it has had on the English people – as if that were all to the good. No one pointed out that there was also a deleterious side. The primitive tribes of the Middle East, like all such people, were a savage, bloodthirsty and vengeful lot. The Old Testament is full of this language. Since the Puritans had an obsession with the Bible, particularly with the Old Testament, this language appealed to them and encouraged their brutal instincts.

Down with kings! Curse them! Revenge on opponents and enemies! The prayers and preachings of the Saints are full of this kind of thing, their language of the bowels, of blood and blood-sacrifice, cleansing by the shedding of blood. In seventeenth-century circumstances it all had an appalling influence.

It might have been much better for them if they read the plays of Shakespeare – as we know the cultivated King did during his confinement at Holdenby. He read them in the Second Folio produced shortly before the troubles, and made intelligent comments in the margins. But few Puritans could endure stage-plays, condemned as sinful. True, Milton appreciated them in his younger happier years, before he saw the light that blinded him.

Another aspect of the Bible's influence was the prophetic – the encouragement it gave to people's political expectations, dreams and fantasies. In a time of social and religious upheaval these were boundless, and equally ludicrous. Two books in particular encouraged their nonsense, the book of Daniel in the Old Testament, and the book of Revelations in the New. According to Daniel there were four successive world empires – Babylon, the Medes and Persians, Greece, and Rome. (I fear these people had not then the advantage of reading the *Cambridge Ancient History*.) All these had crashed, but now would succeed a Fifth Monarchy that would endure for ever (Daniel VII). This of course would be their own.

'I shall not prophesy if I say, The sword is now drawn, whose anger shall not be pacified till Babylon be down, and Zion raised.' They would raise it by the sword. In such a time of upheaval it was open to the butcher, the baker and the candlestick-maker to hold forth in the Army and the pulpits on such topics. And not only they. Many people were more than touched by these millenarian expectations, and thought that the English were a Chosen People to be experiencing such thrills.

'Methinks I see in my mind,' wrote Milton, 'a noble and puissant nation rousing herself like a strong man after sleep. Methinks I see her as an eagle mewing her mighty youth, and kindling her undazzled eyes at the full midday beam.' No idea that, specifically, their eyes were dazzled by events. Again, 'Let not England forget her precedence of teaching nations how to live.' Again, God was revealing Himself, as was his manner, 'first to His Englishmen'.

These notions went along with a naif nationalism. All revolutions go through what Lenin called an 'infantile disease' – the Russian Revolution had its apocalyptic expectations; so had the French. The Puritan Revolution in England naturally thought in terms of its Bible mania.

Thomas Harrison was a lower-class man, the son of a Staffordshire butcher. The snobbish Lucy Hutchinson, who came of a *very* good family, regarded him as having the crudities and vanities of a self-made man, who had risen above himself to a position of wealth and influence as one of Cromwell's Major-Generals. Richard Baxter, an educated fellow, regarded him as 'a man of excellent natural parts for affection and oratory, but not well seen in the principles of his religion'. This meant that he was not a Presbyterian like Baxter. 'Of a sanguine complexion, naturally of such a vivacity, hilarity and alacrity as another man hath when he hath drunken a cup too much. But naturally also so far from humble thoughts of himself that it was his ruin.'

One was supposed to humble oneself, or at least make a show of doing so – no one was better at that than Oliver Cromwell. That is why so many thought the great man an imposter. Harrison who followed him hopefully was more than a bit above himself: in other words, lower-class manners.

It was typical that at the time when Parliament was to be purged, clever Ireton used the underdog to make a temporary truce with the Levellers, since Harrison was closer to them. Moreover he was notoriously moral. When later a fellow Regicide, Gregory Clement, was discovered in bed with his maidservant, Harrison had him expelled from Parliament and the company of the Saints. For good measure Clement's signature was expunged from the death-warrant – one could not have that sanctified document polluted.

Like Cromwell, Harrison urged Parliament to use victory to 'improve this Mercy in establishing the ways of righteousness, and opening a wider door to the publishing the everlasting Gospel'. He got his chance when he became President of the Commission for the Propagation of the Gospel in Wales. This devoted itself to removing 'scandalous', i.e. royalist, ministers, so the Church in Wales, thus denuded, never recovered. Harrison however did well: he was said to make an income of £2000 a year, and committed the mistake of making a show of it. Oddly enough, the King had no feelings against him, though Harrison took a foremost part in pushing forward the 'trial'. Cromwell too thought him 'an honest man, and aims at good things, yet from the impatience of his spirit will not wait the Lord's leisure, but hurries me on to that which he and all honest men will have cause to repent'.

Harrison never repented of anything, and made himself the leader of the Fifth Monarchy men meeting regularly at All Hallows in the City for 'solemn seeking unto God for the pouring forth of his

Spirit'. Harrison helped Cromwell to kick out Parliament, forcing the Speaker to leave the chair (shades of Charles I's ineffective attempt!), Harrison being 'fully persuaded they had not a heart to do any more good for the Lord and his people'.

Then he broke with Cromwell who, like the statesman he was, wanted peace with Holland, while Harrison and his gang 'do rail and preach every day against the General and the peace with Holland'. He opposed the leader becoming Lord Protector as assuming the sovereignty of God, and once and again had to be put under lock and key. When Roger Williams came over from the New Jerusalem to see how things were getting on, he thought him 'second in the nation of late', advocating a council of seventy, like the biblical Sanhedrim, to run its affairs. This took shape as Praise-God Barebones' Parliament, a comic short-lived experiment. However, Harrison is 'a very gallant, most deserving, heavenly man; but most high-flown from the kingdom of the Saints and the Fifth Monarchy now risen, and their sun never to set again.'

It was shortly to set, but it was for such a paragon of virtue to set a good example when the sun went down.

This he proceeded to do. He made no attempt to abscond as cousin Whalley had done. 'If I had been minded to run away, I might have had many opportunities. But being so clear in the thing, I durst not turn my back nor step a foot out of the way, by reason I had been engaged in the service of so glorious and great a God.'

At his trial he stuck to his convictions defiantly. 'I

believe the hearts of some have felt the terrors of that Presence of God that was with his servants in those days (however it seemeth good to Him to suffer this turn to come on us), and are witnesses that the thing was not done in a corner.' The Regicides, the Cromwellians, were all proud of the fact that the 'trial' and execution of the King were public acts, demonstrations before the opinion of the world. They were men of conviction. Milton made a great point of it when he defended the judgment in his Latin tract for the benefit of European opinion.

'There was more from God than men are aware of ... And whereas it hath been said that we did assume and usurp an authority, I say this was done rather in the Fear of the Lord.' This shocked the court, which protested, 'You are in the assembly of Christians: would you make God the author of your treason and murders? We will allow you to say for your own defence what you can.'

Very well then. 'Divers of those that sit upon the Bench were as active –' At this Judge Annesley protested that he had been one of that 'Corrupt Majority, as they called it' who had been expelled from the House by force in order to bring the King to trial.

Harrison consented to plead to the point of law, that 'this that hath been done was done by a Parliament of England, by the Commons of England assembled in Parliament'. The court rejoined that it was 'not done by one Estate. They were but a part: nay, but an eighth part.' Denzil Holles, who had been one of the extruded – and also one of the opposition whom the King had hoped to catch, if his plan had not been betrayed by the intriguing Lady

Carlisle to Pym – now interrupted to say: 'It was not an House of Commons. They kept up a company by the power of the sword. That House of Commons, which you say gave you authority, you know what yourself made of it when you pulled out the Speaker.'

This was a personal point that went home. Harrison rejoined with another. He had not been one 'to turn, as many did, that did put their hands to this plough'. There some of them were, on the Bench. 'Maybe, I might be a little mistaken, but I did it all according to the best of my understanding, desiring to make the revealed Will of God in his holy Scriptures as a guide to me.' At this the Judge, Sir Orlando Bridgman, had to call for order. 'Gentlemen, this humming is not at all becoming the gravity of this court. Let there be free speaking by the prisoner and counsel. It is more fitting for a stage-play than for a court of justice.'

And so the exchanges went on. It has been observed how fair the proceedings were, especially for a seventeenth-century trial. The reason for this is political. The Restoration rested upon the alliance, at last, of Parliament with the monarchy. Neither Charles II nor Clarendon was a vindictive man – unlike the Puritans – and the government had to tread cautiously. The trial had to be seen to be fair. The Regicides were allowed to speak up for themselves, for their guilt was not in doubt.

Hence the ghastly sentence pronounced for treason – we may quote it once to serve for all. 'You shall be drawn upon a hurdle to the place of execution, and there you shall be hanged by the neck and, being alive, shall be cut down and your privy members to be cut off, your entrails to be taken out of your body and (you living) the same to be burnt before your eyes; and your head to be cut off, your body to be divided into four quarters, and your head and quarters to be disposed of at the pleasure of the King's Majesty. And the Lord have mercy on your soul.'

The sentence was duly carried out at Charing Cross, and 'he hanged with his face looking towards the Banqueting House at Whitehall', where the King had suffered. We will go into no more details – one can only hope that the man was unconscious before the further barbarities were committed upon his body. 'His head is since set on a pole on the top of the south-east end of Westminster Hall, looking towards London. The quarters of his body are in like manner exposed upon some of the City gates.'

Such was the butchery of the seventeenth century. But this enlightened age has witnessed worse at Belsen, Auschwitz, and many other places.

Supported by his beliefs, Harrison took his sentence, and endured his sufferings cheerfully. Taunted by the mob as to the whereabouts now of the Good Old Cause, he smiled and said, clapping his hand on his breast, 'Here it is and I am going to seal it with my blood.' Here indeed it was, his own mere afflatus. He was firmly convinced that there would be a reversal of events, and that the rule of the Saints would yet be restored. His group of Fifth Monarchy fools reported that he was soon to rise again, judge his judges, and restore the kingdom of the Saints. The Royalist Cowley made a comedy of it in *The Cutter of Coleman Street* (a Puritan hot-bed).

4. Fifth Monarchy Fanatics

Among the Fifth Monarchy fanatics some held that laughter was a sin, though 'when the Ancient of days shall sit down upon a burning fiery throne ... then the godly shall Laugh it amain' – i.e. they shall have the last laugh, though one would not have thought a burning fiery throne comfortable for the posteriors even of the Ancient of days. No sense of humour anywhere in their voluminous literature. Naturally enough, for their aim was 'to enforce discipline upon the masses'. Nor did they hold with the Levellers that sovereignty belonged to the people: this was to impeach the sovereignty of Christ.

This was the specific view of **John Carew**, an upper-class man. In the sect he was generally held second to Harrison, though he had not the excuse of his low, butcherly origins. For Carew belonged to the widespread clan of Norman descent, himself the grandson of the delightful Cornish antiquary, Richard Carew of Antony.

Somewhere along the line lugubrious Puritanism came in, perhaps from the neighbours. Not far away, at St Germans – monastic property – was the home of the Parliamentarian demagogue, Sir John Eliot, regarded as a martyr, for his feverish consumptive body slept in the Tower. Next door were the Puritan Rouses of Halton, of whom the learned Francis Rous wrote the Puritans' doggerel version of the Psalms, while a step-son was the redoubtable John Pym.

Carew's half-brother, Sir Alexander, was affected by these Parliamentarian persuasions and leaned to that side. He then thought better of it and, when the Royalists were winning in the West, tried to procure the surrender of Plymouth to them. For this Parliament had him executed on Tower Hill. His much younger brother, whose convictions were stronger, indeed steely, would not plead for pardon for him. At Antony a fine portrait of Alexander Carew has at some time been cut out of its frame. Who more likely to have committed this depredation than the uncompromising brother? One sees the stitches where later it was repaired.

John Carew was educated at Oxford, Gloucester Hall (now Worcester College), and then at Inner Temple. He was twenty-one at the time of his brother's disgrace, and three years later was forked into the Long Parliament as a 'recruiter' member for Tregony. He does not appear to have fought in the Army, with him religious belief was a full-time job. He had no difficulty in being recruited either to the High Court of Justice and signing the death warrant – he at least never claimed otherwise, he was proud of his deviation.

Within the sect he had an associate in the notorious Anna Trapnell. A shipwright's daughter, she took to having visions, lying in bed for days in trances. Visited by numerous credulous fools in this time of upheaval, successful publicity turned her head and she became the prophetess of the sect. Nothing would shut Anna Trapnell's trap, though she did not claim – as at least two of the womenfolk did, that they were pregnant by the Holy Ghost and would give birth to the Messiah.

Twice this lady visited Carew in Cornwall on her tour of the West, though I do not know whether she was with him when he set up a church for the Fifth Monarchy lunatics at Exeter. They opposed Cromwell's elevation as Protector, and when he locked them up John Carew went to him to protest. The

1. Charles I at his Trial, by Edward Bower.

2. Oliver Cromwell, by Robert Walker.

3. Henry Ireton, miniature by Samuel Cooper.

4. Thomas Harrison,
by Van de Gucht.

5. Edmund Ludlow.

6. John Bradshaw and Hugh Peters.

7. Lord Grey of Groby.

8. Henry Marten,
by Sir Peter Lely.

9. John Milton, by
William Faithorne.

Gul. Faithorne ad Vivum   *Delin. et sculpsit.*

Ioannis Miltoni Effigies Ætat: 62.
1670.

10. Colonel Hutchinson.

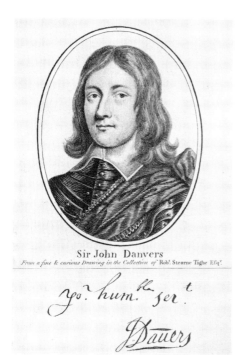

Sir John Danvers

From a fine & curious Drawing in the Collection of Rob. Stearne Tighe Esq*.

11. Sir John Danvers.

12. Colonel Pride.

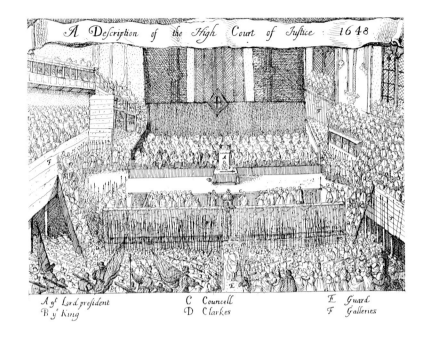

A Description of the High Court of Justice 1648

A y^e Lord president   C Councell   E Guard
B y^e King   D Clarkes   F Galleries

13. The Trial of Charles I.

WITHAL

14. The Execution of Charles I.

good politician told him that he was imprisoning them not for religion, but for sedition. Carew himself wrote a tract against the Protectorate, *The Grand Catastrophe or the Change of Government*. He wrote under the signature, J. Cornubiensis, 'There are those who suspect you'll *King* it, and procure your *Heir* to succeed you.' This was a shrewd hit. Oliver Cromwell gave him a spell in Pendennis Castle, to cool his heels if not his brain.

Some of these people saw the Protector as the Little Horn of the book of Daniel. He should be smitten with all force. They argued that it was no sin to kill Cromwell, and the lower-class Venner prepared for a rising. Carew was not prepared for this – an upper-class man he wanted social anarchy no more than Cromwell did. When the great man died, and their world was breaking down around their ears, Harrison and Carew re-baptised themselves in the water at the Tower. I suspect the point of this was that they were making a deal with the Baptists.

John Carew had no thought of escaping, as others had. Was it not written in the book of Revelations, XX.4, 'And I saw the souls of them that were beheaded for the witness of Jesus, and for the Word of God, and which had not worshipped the Beast. And they lived and reigned with Christ a thousand years.' He would be one of these. He waited patiently at Looe, whence he could easily have shipped across-Channel. That was not his intention: he would be a witness that he had 'committed both his life and his estate to the Lord, to save or destroy as He thought meet'.

A Puritan account of Carew's travails tells us that

all the way up to London 'he had a gracious presence
of the Lord with him. Otherwise the many
reproaches and hard usage in the way had been
sufficient to have troubled his spirit.' In most towns
people greeted him with 'Hang him, Rogue', 'Pistol
him'. At Salisbury they recommended hanging him
at the next signpost without any further trouble.
'This is the rogue will have no king but Jesus.
Indeed, the rage of the people all the way was such
that, had he not been indued with strength from on
High, he could not have undergone the wicked and
barbarous deportment and carriage of the giddy
multitude.' It brings home to us that Puritans never
represented the ordinary, normal people: they
formed a morose and disagreeable minority.

The trial followed the usual course, we may omit
the formalities. The Judge offered politely, 'Mr
Carew, if you will have pen, ink and paper, you may
have it. Pray call for it.' Carew: 'I have no need of it.'
His speech ended, 'I can say in the presence of the
Lord, who is the searcher of all hearts, that what I
did was in His fear, and I did it in obedience to His
holy and righteous laws.'

At that, we are told, *'Here the people hummed.'*
The Judge had to intervene to get him a hearing: 'Go
on, you shall not be interrupted.' Carew went on
with a long speech that obedience to the Lord was
the chief thing, secondly obedience to the supreme
authority of the nation. Lawyer-like, Carew went on
and on arguing the point, and was as often
questioned, until lawyer Annesley interposed, 'that
which you pretend is by authority is no authority;
for a few of you set up an arbitrary Parliament of a
few of yourselves, when you had driven away the

rest.' Annesley had himself been one of those excluded.

There was no disputing that, and at last Carew agreed that he had signed both the death-warrant, and that for summoning the High Court. All in the fear of the Lord, and 'I am willing to leave it with the Lord'. Even the equable, and equitable, Judge Bridgman was driven to protest, '*In nomine domini, in the name of the Lord* all mischiefs have been done.'

An unkind Royalist comment was, 'It is no wonder that he was one of the Judges of the King, who was consenting to the death of his own brother.'

John Carew took his own death cheerfully enough. 'Coming down Newgate stairs to go into the sledge, in a very smiling and cheerful manner, his countenance shining with great glory, he uttered words to this effect: "My Lord Jesus endured the Cross, whose steps I desire to follow." ' A Royalist newspaper, however, accounted for his shining face by his having drunk three pints of sack [sherry] 'to bear up his spirits', which flushed his face and put him into such a sweat that his handkerchief could not quench it.

By Charles II's favour to the family his quarters were not disposed about the City, but allowed to his relations for private burial.

Few tracks of his life remain of him in his native Cornwall – no doubt the family at Antony did not wish to publicise this black sheep any further. When loyalist MPs were disabled from Parliament he was shoved in for Tregony, and in 1646 was one of the commissioners sent to receive the King upon his confinement at Holdenby. He served regularly on Parliament's Navy Committee 1646–52.

After his rigid attendance at the High Court, he

was a member of the Commonwealth's Councils of State 1651–3. In Praise-God Barebones' assembly of the righteous, 1653, he sat to represent Devon. An utter doctrinaire in politics as in religion, he opposed Cromwell's elevation as Protector, was summoned before his Council and imprisoned for a while in charming St Mawes castle, on the opposite side of Falmouth harbour to more commodious Pendennis. In 1658 he was under restraint again briefly, but, on Oliver's death, was summoned to the restored Rump – then fined £100. Was this for non-attendance? Evidently a *mauvais coucheur*.

At the Restoration the Commons excluded him from the Act of Indemnity by 80 votes against 70. It is interesting that there were so many to favour him. However, he was a gentleman of family, who had never made a penny from his deviation – and many must have known him in public affairs, if not in the last fatal assembly. There, when bidden to plead, he had insisted, 'Saving to our Lord Jesus Christ's right to the government of these kingdoms', and of course, he had done everything 'in the fear of the holy and righteous Lord, the Judge of the Earth'. Nothing could be done with such a type.

When he died he was thirty-seven or thirty-eight. A wasted life.

CHAPTER 5

Escapees

Of the 59 pure Regicides only nine underwent the death penalty, plus three or four non-signatories. A number escaped abroad, though a few were brought back to receive their due. The great majority got off with imprisonment. Tribute to the comparative clemency of the Restoration – for that time. Neither Charles II nor Clarendon was inspired by the vengeful spirit of Bible mania, as Puritans were.

Of the escapees **Edmund Ludlow** was the most prominent, regarded as such by hopeful spirits expecting a reversal of fate. For he lived on to a ripe old age – long enough to come back at the Revolution of 1688, a sober take-over by Dutch William from foolish James II, who threw everything away (including the Great Seal into the Thames, as if that did him any good!). In the sensible circumstances of William III's new deal the republican Ludlow found that he wasn't wanted, and went back to die in Switzerland in 1692.

Ludlow was born of Wiltshire gentry, his mother of the Phillips family of beautiful Montacute, that yet remains to our delight. At Trinity College, Oxford he was engaged once in philosophical

69

disputation with the irascible old President Kettel. It was about the nonsense-issue whether the things one sees are *real*, or not. The old Doctor provided an illustration for the obstinate lad who would not take telling. 'The fox wagging his tail and, seeing its shadow upon the wall, said it was an horn. Was that an horn?' 'Yes,' said Ludlow, 'it was a horn, a *real* horn.' 'Then toot it, you fool, you,' said old Kettel.

This was typical of Ludlow, people thought there was something wooden about him – Carlyle sharply called him a 'wooden-head'. Oliver Cromwell thought him so too. Sitting beside him in Parliament one day, Cromwell whispered to him, 'These men will never leave till the Army pull them out by the ears!' Here was the origin of Pride's Purge, though Cromwell was too astute to take the responsibility for it: he left the obloquy of it to Colonel Pride, whose name has disgraced it ever since.

Once, years later, when the believing republican went to protest against Cromwell's becoming Lord Protector, the great man threw a cushion at the wooden-head. No arguing with it.

Ludlow was noted to be no speaker or preacher, but joined up at once to fight ardently for the Good Old Cause. As such he played an effective part in his native Wiltshire, and was pushed into Parliament as a 'recruiter' in 1646 to represent it. There he chummed up with Henry Marten from neighbouring Berkshire. Both belonged to the radical Republican wing, and pushed forward the Purge, and the King's 'trial'. There Ludlow observed the King's dignity and usual impassibility: 'he looked with as impudent a face as if he had not been guilty of the blood that hath been shed in this war.' Charles himself did not recognise any responsibility for it. Of course. When he was charged as 'traitor and murderer' he merely smiled.

At the Restoration Ludlow hung about Westminster for some days wondering whether to take advantage of the Act of Indemnity. He employed the interval usefully arranging his affairs, evidently laying in a stock of money for his flight, for he never at any time seems to have been hard up. Discretion became the better part of valour, and one dark night he made his way through 'James's' Fields – no Saint would say 'St' James. He made his way via the City and then by back roads over the Downs, being helped by godly persons and also by growing a beard to disguise himself. And so to the Sussex coast, whence he got a shallop across to Dieppe.

He did not think much of Paris, where he was kindly looked after by a Huguenot family – especially one day at the Palais Royal, at the elevation of the Host, where he was much put to it to avoid the 'idolizing thereof'. Another time he turned his back upon it, 'the baser sort reviling me' for it in the street. He managed to get a horse to take him to Lyons, where he fell in with a party of the Reformed Religion, (*Prétendue Réformée* to Catholics), and got safely to the haven of Geneva. (Servetus had not been so lucky at the vindictive hands of Calvin, who had him burned, though no Catholic. He was not 'orthodox' enough, and had leanings towards rationality.)

In Switzerland Ludlow learned from the gazettes the news of affairs in England, and also received regular supplies of money. He was good at protecting himself, and negotiating with the authorities at Berne for his security. He seems to have had a good time, for he kept hounds for hunting and several fine horses. He also employed himself writing reams of reminiscences justifying himself and celebrating the martyrs for the Good Old Cause. He was quite unrepentant, never allowed that there was another side to things, of course.

The martyred Harrison had been waiting for 'the accomplishment of those promises that relate to the setting up of the sceptre of Jesus Christ [he could go on waiting], neglecting no means he judged conducing to the great end'. He had been ready for any and every means, but found himself mistaken, 'a little mistaken, maybe', he said at his trial. God had so clearly witnessed to the rightness of their cause, 'not only by his Word, but by a series of providences writing his approbation thereof, as it were by the beams of the sun'. That is, they were justified simply by success. They all thought like that. Then how about when the beams of the sun were withdrawn? Ludlow had his explanation pat: it 'spoke the chastising of us for not improving the Mercies of the Lord as we ought'. They should have gone further. Here was the spirit that merited retribution and required repression.

'But God will not be mocked, for though – as David prophesied, Psalms 2, 2, 3 – the kings of the earth set themselves, and the rulers take counsel together against the Lord, saying "Let us break their bonds asunder." Yet, saith the Prophet, verses 4, 5, 6, "He that sits in the heavens shall laugh, the Lord shall have them in derision".' Thus these fools consoled themselves. But they expected to see another day. Ludlow tells us that Harrison died 'in full assurance of the resurrection of this cause, and said What he had done, if it were to be done again he would do it'. We see that these people required to be dealt with.

Of Ludlow's writing we learn, 'spiritual intensity and apocalyptic prophecy are closely woven into the narrative, and give it its guiding purpose. Political events, inseparable in Ludlow's mind from their millenarian context, are to him the workings of the God who "shakes nations", "levels mountains", "overturns, overturns", and prepares for the destruction of the Beast ... Ludlow brings out the entire providence detection-kit to show that the destruction of the Anti-Christian régime is inevitable: storms, comets, plagues, fires, ghost armies fighting in the sky [cf. *Paradise Lost*, Books V and VI], huge whales [Leviathans] washed up on beaches, children born with two heads and four arms, millions of whitings swarming on dry land, and so on.' These people would have made suitable companions for the deluded maniacs of Waco, Texas: same breed.

Is it any wonder that the rule of such people should have been succeeded by the scepticism and rationalism of the later seventeenth century? Or by the cynical Charles II's patronage of the Royal Society and experimental science? When the rationalist Toland came to edit Ludlow's Memoirs, at the time of the reasonable solutions attained in 1688, he edited out the credulities and reduced it to sober common sense.

For all the protection Ludlow received in the sanctified city of Geneva, he was not satisfied as to the purity of their religion. 'Neither in doctrine nor discipline, principle nor practice, they have made such progress since the time of the first Reformation as might have been hoped for, but have rather gone backward and brought forth sour grapes.' By this time he was joined by two more of the Saints or, rather, Regicides and a clerk of the High Court, Andrew Broughton. William Cawley went under the alias W. Johnson, John Lisle under that of J. Ralpheson, Ludlow under his mother's name of Phillips.

Though they attended the preachments in church, 'we had not a freedom to communicate with any in that holy ordinance of the Lord's Supper of whom we had not a particular satisfaction of a work of grace in their hearts, and that their conversation was suitable thereto'. This was pretty offensive coming from guests and supplicants. They had been taken under the wing of a Pastor Hummel, who replied that the rule was that all who were not excommunicated should communicate. So they departed further down the lake, Cawley and Lisle to Lausanne, Ludlow to Vevey, where no doubt they were freer to follow their blessed consciences than at Geneva.

William Cawley was the son of a wealthy brewer of Chichester, educated at Hart Hall, now Hertford College, Oxford and at Gray's Inn. Though a supposedly educated man, he was one of the commissioners for 'demolishing superstitious pictures and monuments in London'. The artistic damage they did was enormous – and unforgivable. Even Henry Marten objected to their wrecking the Queen's chapel at Somerset House, where they threw the magnificent Rubens altarpiece into the Thames. The splendid stained glass of Henry VII's chapel in Westminster, equal to that of King's College chapel at Cambridge, by the same makers, was destroyed. And so they went through the City and Westminster, as other miscreants went through counties and cities elsewhere.[1]

Cawley religiously attended every meeting of the spurious High Court of Justice, and duly signed up. A big nob in Chichester, he was well placed for buying up Royalist property. He bought one manor near Hastings that had belonged to Lord Craven, and two belonging to the Crown near Chichester. By the time he arrived in Switzerland he was elderly and infirm. Negotiations went to and fro with the authorities to give them warrant and protection. Ludlow relates them with his usual long-windedness. When their warrant came through Cawley excused himself from waiting on their Excellencies: 'a wide and incurable rupture in the intestines with a spice of the stone modestly pleads my excuse.' However, he was not too infirm to plead the case of 'the stripped and peeled exiles', who had done the Lord's work in demolishing idols, 'executing judgment on malefactors, ejecting lordly domineering prelates, profane and scandalous ministers, dumb dogs, shepherds who understood not', etc. We remember that this is the language of Milton's 'Lycidas':

> Blind mouths! that scarce themselves know how to hold
> A sheep-hook, or have learned aught else the least

---

[1] Cf. my *Reflections on the Puritan Revolution, passim*.

That to the faithful herdsman's art belongs ...
The hungry sheep look up and are not fed.

However, rupture or not, Cawley lived on at Vevey till 1667, though 'stripped and peeled' of his ill-gotten gains.

John Lisle was of superior social standing, being a younger son of a knight in the Isle of Wight. He was said to have had an unhappy childhood, a father who drank, but whom he eventually got out of the estate and pensioned off. Graduating from Oxford – Magdalen Hall (now Hertford College) followed by Middle Temple – he made a rich marriage to a daughter of the Puritan Hobart, Lord Chief Justice. On her death he married another heiress who, as Alice Lisle, became a famous martyr for aiding and abetting the Somerset rebels in Monmouth's Rebellion.

This equipped him to take a prominent part in the King's 'trial', as Bradshaw's assistant, and to become a commissioner of the Great Seal. As such he preened himself as 'Chancellor of England' among the Swiss, impressed by this and 'charmed by his religious devotion'. He had money, for he did well out of Crown property, and had a desirable country residence as Master of St Cross Hospital near Winchester. In revolutions it is not the meek who inherit the earth.

In Switzerland the exiles still needed protection, and shortly a couple of Irish Catholics turned up at first at Vevey, then at Lausanne. It seems that they were really after Ludlow, who had been Cromwell's second-in-command in subjugating Ireland. Ludlow sent warning to Lisle to forbear going publicly to church while these suspicious fellows were hanging about. Lisle did not heed the advice: his life was in the hand of God; he had committed himself entirely to His protection. Moreover, 'till our enemies had dispatched me [Ludlow], he assured himself they would not think of him'.

Was this just Ludlow's usual conceit? Anyway, since the desperados couldn't get him, they got Lisle. As he was parading to church to hear the sermon, he 'was shot dead by a person on foot, who had a companion waiting for him on horseback with a led horse; which the murderer having mounted and cried "Vive le Roi", they immediately got away through the nearby towngate.' The assassin was known as a MacDonnell, but his real name seems to have been MacCartain.

Nicholas Love was luckier than his fellow Hampshire MP, Lisle: he joined the group at Vevey and survived safely there into old age. He was a lawyer and a Wykehamist, indeed the son of the Head Master of Winchester, canon of the cathedral. What can have bitten him?

From Wadham College, Oxford, he went on to Lincoln's Inn. As a barrister he became Recorder of Basingstoke, and Parliament made him one of the six clerks of Chancery, which brought him a heap of money. With his background he was able to make hay while the sun shone out of the large estates of the see of Winchester. However, when the Parliamentary army occupied the city, he prevented them from destroying the buildings of the College. For this much must be forgiven him.

At the 'Trial' too he had a better record than most. Though called in by the Army officers to draft the charge, he opposed the King's execution. He pleaded for delay and further consideration. This was very unpopular with those who were hurrying it on. Indeed the speed of events, and the blatant publicity of it all, took people's breath away, and amazed Europe.

This event frightened away **John Say**, who had meanwhile joined the exiles. He fled into Germany, and eventually found safety at Amsterdam, when war broke out between England and Holland. Thence he wrote to Ludlow to come and take a lead among the faithful once more. 'Believe me, things are so well prepared here to answer the good ends we all desire that nothing seems to be wanting but hands to set the wheels going. Invitations and encouragements are not only offered but pressed upon you.' Evidently Ludlow was looked upon as the leader overseas, and hopes of his taking up the command continued to be held at home by adherents of the Good Old Cause.

Lisle begged Ludlow to come to Holland, 'I am certainly informed that considerable numbers in England, Scotland and Ireland will appear for us. And such measures will be taken here for their assistance that I have great hopes of success.' This was not the usual fantasy of exiles; for Holland was at war with England. This meant that these people were enemies of their country. Ludlow did not think well of the prospects, but the matter gives us a longer perspective in which to view William of Orange's invasion in 1688.

5. Escapees

William Say died luckily, and peacefully, in Holland. A lawyer, his mother was a daughter of a judge. He was another Oxford man – shocking how many of the Regicides were Oxford men. It gives point to Hobbes's objection to the study of the classics at university, with so much talk of republican virtue, civil war and sedition, depositions, political assassinations, the cult of 'tyrannicide'. Say graduated from University College, thence to Middle Temple. He did not take part in the fighting, but in acquiring the sequestered estates of Lord Abergavenny. He acted as temporary president at the King's trial, until the arrival of Bradshaw, and thereafter sat on the left hand of on high. He drafted the death-warrant, and reported the proceedings to what remained of the Commons. On their behalf he shortly tried the Levellers, who had raised a riot in the Fens, where he had been a speculator in enclosing. Evidently no friend to social disruption, as attorney of the Marshal's Court he drew profits 'which should perhaps have gone to the state'.

By the autumn of 1662 there were considerable additions to the exiles in Switzerland. Not only Say, but **Andrew Broughton** and **John Phelps**, who had been clerks at the High Court, and **Edward Dendy**, serjeant-at-arms there. There were also **Cornelius Holland, Nicholas Love,** Colonel Biscoe and Slingsby Bethel, the prolific pamphleteer. Holland and Love were Regicides, but Love, though attending, had not thought fit to sign.

Some of these have their Latin memorials in the church at Vevey, where I have scrambled before now down behind the backs of the raised wooden pews to read them. Andrew Broughton of Maidstone lived on to the ripe old age of eighty-four, dying in 1687/8. Cawley died in January, 1666/7, aged sixty-three; Nicholas Love in 1682, aged seventy-four. Ludlow, who died in 1693, has the longest-winded inscription, which recites his record and tells us that he had the company of his wife in exile. John Phelps received a much later memorial, in English, from his descendants in New Jersey and Massachusetts, where Puritan humbug lasted longest: he was 'an exile in the cause of human freedom'.

Holland proved no such safe harbour for the Regicides as they thought. Downing, the ex-Cromwellian, who had become Charles II's envoy, bullied the States into extraditing the three, Barkstead, Corbet and Okey. Downing was a harsh fellow, mean and grasping. The great French minister, Colbert, called him 'le plus grand querrelleur de tous les diplomates de l'Europe'. But he got his men.

Little Mr Pepys saw the three drawn by, as he stood by a draper's shop at the corner of Aldgate: he thought 'they all looked very cheerful'. But he had no good opinion of the ex-Cromwellian Downing for rounding them up. 'The Dutch were a good while before they could be persuaded to let them go. All the world takes notice of him for a most ungrateful villain for his pains.'

John Barkstead was a pure Cromwellian. A London goldsmith and silversmith by profession, he joined up at once to fight, and was wounded several times.

5. Escapees

He took part in the shameful sack of Basing House, a double palace of treasures, medieval castle and Elizabethan mansion, of the Catholic Marquis of Winchester. It was packed with works of art, paintings, plate, tapestries. At the surrender the greatest artist of the time, Inigo Jones – who had built the Banqueting House in Whitehall and the Queen's House at Greenwich – was brought forth, old and ill, naked in a blanket. At Basing now nothing remains but rubble.

In the High Court Barkstead was one of the hard core of Army officers who constituted the judges, for it was an essentially Army affair. He served Cromwell's purposes faithfully, and became one of his Major-Generals, an abortive experiment for governing and disciplining the unsettled country. Barkstead's province was his native Middlesex, where the Puritan severity of his administration of London was bitterly resented and long remembered. He kept down the popular sports of bear-baiting and cock-fighting, and spoiled another popular sport by rounding up some hundreds of prostitutes. One sees why Charles II's reign witnessed such a reaction.

For his services Cromwell, resuming to himself royal prerogatives, knighted him – Sir John Barkstead. To begin with he fled to Lutheran Hanau in Germany – where he was welcomed and given the freedom of the town. He then made the mistake of crossing into Holland to meet his wife, and there he was caught.

So too was **Miles Corbet**. He was of a knightly Norfolk family, and thus educated at Cambridge. At Milton's Puritanical Christ's College he came under the influence of one of the loud-mouthed preachers in the place, John Preston. He took a leading part in organising the formidable Eastern Association. As chairman of the Parliamentary Committee for Ejecting Scandalous (Puritan semantics for Anglican) Ministers, he 'incurred great enmity because of the absolute and to some extent capricious authority' which he wielded.

Though too busy dismissing clergymen from their livings to attend the High Court, he came in for the sentencing and signing. He served Cromwell's régime in Ireland, but – boasting of his integrity in not buying Crown or Church lands – he overlooked his extensive acquisitions over there. To Puritans that was fair game after the unforgotten Massacre of 1641.

John Okey was of humble origin, from Brogborough in Bunyan's (or Bunnion's) Bedfordshire. Drayman, stoker in a brewhouse, then chandler, he naturally jumped at the chance of army service and did well as a soldier. He fought at Naseby and took part in the reduction of various towns and Royalist strongholds. He served under Cromwell in squashing the Levellers at Burford, and was given an honorary M.A. at Oxford, when the great man paid a friendly visit as Chancellor and played bowls at Magdalen. (Can one see Laud doing anything of the sort? He had no gift for popularity. Oliver Cromwell had.)

However, Okey did not approve of Cromwell's becoming Protector, and was now and again under arrest for protesting or forwarding petitions against it. As the Lord Protector got older he lost patience with the opposition of Radicals, Lilburne and such, which he bore patiently on the way up. One wonders whether, in his chair of state, having to dismiss Parliaments, etc., he may not have had some sympathy for the King and what he had had to put up with.

Okey did well, for a lower-class man, out of the Revolution. He was awarded Scottish lands worth £300 a year, and in his native county he was enabled to buy Brogborough Park, the estate of the gentry in his parish, as well as lands at Ampthill and Leighton Buzzard.

In Holland he moved about under the alias of Frederick Williamson. It did not save him from the attentions of Downing.

All three of these miscreants had not submitted to the Act of Indemnity, and so were *ipso facto* guilty and required no trial. They suffered the death penalty. On the scaffold Barkstead declared himself a Congregationalist, i.e. an old-style Army Independent, no stuck-up Presbyterian he. Okey held forth with pious ejaculations, which Ludlow retails at length. We need not go into them: we now know them well enough – all according to form.

Because, also on the scaffold, Okey had the sense to recommend to his old comrades submission to the existing government, Charles II granted his wife permission for Okey's private burial; while the Duke of York returned to her enough of his property for her maintenance.

Sentences continued to be carried out for years into Charles II's happy reign. In February 1662 the Dutch artist, Schellinks, went along to Tyburn with thousands of other folk to see one such spectacle. These horrid spectacles were immensely popular, and crowds attended them for the fun – more demotic than a stage play. A popular distich of the time reminds us that there was another side to the proceedings: government realised their minatory, or admonitory, effect in keeping order among the *plebs*.

'We walked with thousands of people to Tyburn, and saw there Lord Monson, Sir Henry Mildmay and Mr Wallop lying in their tabards [prison coats] on a little straw on a hurdle being dragged through under the gallows, where some articles were read to them and then torn up. After that they were again dragged through the town back to the Tower. Their sentence is that they are to be dragged through under the gallows on this day every year.'[2]

Well, this outing in (not very) fresh air was better than death anyway.

Monson was let off death because he withdrew from the High Court before the end, and did not sign the death warrant. As a pretty boy he had been dressed up, powdered and posseted, to attract the attentions of the susceptible James I. His backers evidently did not understand the facts of life, for James liked masculine, not feminine, types. Monson went on to a normal, but complicated, matrimonial life. He married the rich widow of Lord Admiral Howard, of Armada fame. They lived at Reigate Castle, which he held against Lord Holland in the Second Civil War, until relieved by fellow Regicide, Sir Michael Livesey. Monson's third wife was a virago, who used to wallop him. A royalist newsprint mocked him: '*Ordered* – that the Lord Monson have a privilege to wear a back-piece,

[2] *The Journal of William Schellinks' Travels in England, 1661–1663*. Trans. and ed. M. Exwood and H.L. Lehmann. Camden Soc., 1993, 72, 82–3, 86.

breast-plate, and a pot, to secure his bones from the knocks of his Lady's bed-staff.'

He was a cousin of the Wallops. The poor fellow eventually died in the Fleet prison.

Robert Wallop was a cousin also of the Corbets. Another renegade from Hart Hall, Oxford, he attended the High Court only three times, and did not sign up. At his own trial he professed that he had sat 'only at the request of his Majesty's friends, in order to try to moderate their furious proceedings'. This got him off death. It is evident that Charles II's government did not want to have too many of these executions on their hands. Wallop had a grant of £10,000 – a nominal sum – out of the confiscated estates of the Marquis of Winchester, who had defended Basing House so courageously, and, in my view, mistakenly – or that stately treasure dome might have been left to us.

Sir Henry Mildmay had been educated at his grand-father's Puritan foundation, Emmanuel, at Cambridge. He followed that up by the drastic measure of sending his son to Harvard, where no less than eleven of the original Fellows were Emmanuelites. It was this, his religious formation, that put him wrong; for socially he was conservative, a grasping, acquisitive type. He had even been a royal official, Master of the Jewel House. It was not very *chic* of him to denounce Charles I's last Treaty with Parliament, declaring that he was 'no more to be trusted than a lion that hath been caged, and let loose again at his liberty'. Perhaps he knew. At his trial Charles had his retort, referring to Mildmay as 'my jewel'.

Mildmay's large acquisitions were confiscated, and he died while being transported later to Tangier.

At the end of April 1662 Schellinks was able to view the full proceedings at Tyburn, executed upon the three malefactors Downing had rounded up in Holland.

There was such an immense crowd of people and the throng was so great that the sheriffs were forced to take the malefactors from the sledges and lead them to the cart, which stood already waiting under the gallows.

On the way Barkstead was eating or chewing something, Okey had an orange in his hand, and Corbet a book, but he was kept from reading by the shouting and mud-slinging crowds. The hangman took off Barkstead's wig and put the noose round his neck; this was hauled so tight that he could not sit on the side of the cart; as he was too weak to stand the hangman said, 'You shall have plenty of rope', and made it a little wider so that he could sit down. He then took out a silver flask and drank a cordial.

Okey was the next to be put on the cart. Barkstead said to him, 'Welcome, brother.' Whereupon Okey, seeing him without his wig, embraced him with both arms, and said, 'Mr Sheriff, I hope we shall have the liberty to speak and to pray.' Then Corbet was brought on to the cart and Okey, who showed himself very courageous and of good spirits, addressed the Sheriff and the people with a long oration. After him spoke Miles Corbet, and then Barkstead who, because of his weakness, made it short. Then Corbet began to pray, after him Okey, and then Barkstead.

Then the ropes were well tied above to the gallows, and white linen caps were put over their faces. As they all commended their souls to God, the cart was driven away. They all hung with their faces towards Westminster. Barkstead was the first to be cut down, and quartered on the ground. First his heart was taken out of his body and shown to the people. This was then thrown on to the fire, and the same was done with his intestines.

The same was done with Okey and Corbet, and their quarters were carried in baskets on carts to London, where the quarters of Barkstead and Corbet, having been boiled, were put on the City gates, Corbet's head on the Bridge. Barkstead's head was put on a stake at the Tower towards the water. On the King's order Okey's quarters were buried at Stepney in the presence of such a crowd of people, who went with it, that it was almost impossible to get through with the body.

Such were the people, such was the time. This was the way these things were done. Public executions were public entertainments. And we know from reading Hardy that, far into the nineteenth century, people would flock for miles to see a public hanging.

If the times seem a little uncivilised, in June Schellinks and his friends went to Smithfield to see a young woman burned alive, who had made the mistake of stabbing her husband to death. This was the regular penalty favoured for women who murdered their husbands.

John Hewson escaped Downing by dying first. Anthony Wood described him as 'sometime an honest shoemaker in Westminster'; Clarendon, however, called him 'a fellow who had been an ill shoemaker, afterwards clerk to a brewer of small beer'. The Army gave him the chance, like so many others, to rise. Like other soldiers too he rose into pulpits, pushing out the parson and taking his place. He openly opposed the ordinance of Parliament, dominated by Presbyterians, forbidding this lay usurpation of the minister's function. At Steeple Aston in Oxfordshire Hewson was able to prove the parson an Anti-Christ by thirteen marks of a false prophet. The junior officers in his regiment joined him in holding forth. When in 1647 the Army threatened the City, the Presbyterian authorities were alarmed, for a Royalist newspaper reported that Hewson had 'Od. ends in him'. I do not know whether this was a rude reference to his appearance, for he was a one-eyed man.

He followed Cromwell in Army politics, a key figure in Pride's Purge, and in the Army's threat to the City. He supported Cromwell's becoming Protector, but was angry at Parliament's offer of the Crown: in this Parliament was worse than the Devil, for the Devil offered the kingdom of the world to Christ only once, but Parliament offered it twice to Cromwell.

One sees how close Milton was to their world, the concerns and the idiom of Puritan thought.

5. Escapees

When things were breaking up Hewson had the job of suppressing the mob of apprentices shouting for a free Parliament – as previously they had shouted for the death of Strafford, and panicked the King into leaving Whitehall. Hewson did not hesitate to shoot, and killed and wounded a number. He was rewarded with pasquils and satires on his person, appearance, origins, etc.

Sing Hi Ho Hewson, the State ne'er went upright
Since cobblers could Pray, Preach, Govern and Fight.

This was much to the point.

John Dixwell was lucky to escape to blissful New England. He had at first tried the brethren in Hanau, but thought better of it and went to Massachusetts where people were more godly. He was a Kentish man of Broome Park (later to become celebrated as Kitchener's residence). A younger son, he was active and influential in his county, playing his part on its committees and enjoying the ministrations of the well-named minister Thoroughgood. Religiously Dixwell was an Independent, which recommended him to Cromwell, who made him Governor of Dover Castle.

Escaping abroad, he joined Whalley and Goff in Massachusetts, then made for the stricter religiosity of New Haven. Changing his name to James Davids he was able to live an open and pious life, comfortably and safely. He engaged in a little business, having money from his first wife. He lived on to a good (or bad) old age, not dying until the later, more respectable Revolution, in 1689.

Thomas Challoner was no less fortunate to get away early to Holland, and to die early at Middelburg in 1661, before Downing could get him. Aubrey tells us he was 'bred up in Oxon' [Exeter College], then at Inner Temple. 'He was a well-bred gentleman, and of very good natural parts, and of an agreeable humour. He had the accomplishments of studies at home, and travels in Italy, France and Germany.'

In the Long Parliament he was associated with Henry Marten. And not only politically: they had the same tastes, and both kept women. 'He was as far from a Puritan as the East from the West. He was of the natural religion, and of Henry Marten's gang, and one who loved to enjoy the pleasures of this life. He was (they say) a good scholar, but he wrote nothing that I hear of, only an anonymous pamphlet, *An Account of the Discovery of Moses' Tomb*, which was written very wittily. It did set the wits of all the Rabbis of the [Westminster] Assembly to work, and 'twas a pretty while before the sham was detected.' John Selden used to mock those wiseacres too.

'He had a trick to go sometimes into Westminster Hall in a morning in termtime, and tell some strange story (sham). And would come thither again about 11 or 12 to have the pleasure to hear how it spread. And sometimes it would be altered with additions, he could scarce know it to be his own.' A practical demonstration of people's intelligence.

He was a gay spark like Harry Marten. Oliver

Cromwell, who had none of their weaknesses, sense of humour either, denounced Marten once publicly as a 'whoremaster', and Challoner as a drunkard.

Evidently not all the Regicides were Saints.

Sir Michael Livesey was a Kentish baronet, and influential there from his status and family rather than from character, for he was incompetent and quarrelsome. He was also accused of running away at the engagement upon Cheriton Down (so was the egregious Hazelrig). Overbearing and unpopular as he was, he managed to organise Kent for Parliament. He quarrelled with his general, Sir William Waller, and retaliated on him by detaching the Kentish horse from his command. However, he succeeded in quelling disturbances at Canterbury in the Second Civil War.

This qualified him for a place on the High Court, where he sat every day and signed the death warrant. At the Restoration he got across to the Low Countries. It was reported that he was cut to pieces by a mob of Dutch boors who were set on him as one of the King's murderers, by a gentleman whom Livesey had offended in Kent. But he was reported to have been seen at Arnhem with Colonel Desborough, and then again to have landed at Plymouth. His end is a mystery: no one seems to know for certain what became of him.

Another of the gang who got away to Holland was the Welsh gent, **Thomas Wogan**, from Pembrokeshire; for his service in the field in Wales Cromwell made him governor of Aberystwyth Castle. Then he was made a member of the High

Court, but did not attend much and did not sign the death warrant. In 1651 he was named to another high court to enforce peace in South Wales, where the Puritan régime was highly unpopular.

In 1660 Wogan surrendered in accordance with the Proclamation. Execution was suspended by reason of the doubt how far he was involved in complicity for the King's death. One sees that the Restoration court, under the Lord Chief Baron of the Exchequer, Bridgman, was conscientious – in a different sense from the bloody-minded Puritans.

Wogan was held in York Castle until July 1664, when he managed to escape to Holland, where he was last seen at Utrecht a couple of years later.

Daniel Blagrave made a get-away to Aachen in Germany. The nephew of the Elizabethan mathematician, John Blagrave, Daniel continued some of his uncle's interests. For when Cromwell threatened him in 1651 that he should not sit in the next Parliament, Blagrave consulted his horoscope, 'whether the soldier shall overcome the Parliament, or the Parliament the soldier'. This was in fact the issue. The Army won.

Blagrave was influential in Reading. The offices that he held there enabled him to acquire the fee-farm of the royal manor of Sonning. A commissioner for the Ejection of Scandalous, i.e. Royalist, ministers, he was held to be a strong persecutor of the proper beneficed clergy.

CHAPTER 6

Lawyers and Politicians

Many of the gentry sent their sons to an Inn of Court to get a smattering of law, necessary for running their estates and private affairs, as well as for local administration as JPs. But few professional lawyers as such were involved in the King's 'trial'. The Army officers who were behind it had great difficulty in getting any lawyer to serve their purpose. Out of the question for any of Royalist sympathies, the leading Parliamentary lawyers – Whitelocke and Widdrington, refused; their Serjeant Nicholas, nominated as commissioner, declined it. The Parliamentary judges, St John, Rolle, Wilde, regarded the proceedings as totally irregular, as they were. They were revolutionary, and signalised it as such.

So the Army officers planning it were thrown back on a lawyer of the second, or even the third, rank, a provincial from Cheshire, **John Bradshaw**. Royalists of course mocked his legal competence. On the other hand Milton, who was always partisan and shared his views, praised him. 'All his early life he was sedulously employed in making himself acquainted with the laws of his country, he then practised with singular success and reputation at the bar.' This was not so. Clarendon, himself a lawyer, knew better: 'not much known in Westminster Hall, although of good practice in the chamber.' A fairer judgment.

Bradshaw was a younger son of a respectable country squire, and so had his way to make. He was sent to Gray's Inn, which leaned more to the Parliamentary side than the other inns of court. His practice was chiefly in Cheshire, where Parliament made him Chief Justice in 1647, his province extending into North Wales.

When he accepted, with some reluctance, the horrid assignment to preside over the King's trial, everything was done to give him dignity, and make it worth his while. He was awarded the deanery of Westminster for residence, which he occupied for the rest of his life. Westminster Hall was dressed up with pomp and formality; Bradshaw had a scarlet robe, a guard, also a tall beaver hat lined with steel in case anybody knocked him on the head. To make sure, the Hall was lined with soldiers, as were the streets around. A completely Army affair.

The affair turned into a duel betwen the King and the 'Lord President', who was frustrated by the prisoner's refusal to plead, at each of the three sessions. The King reiterated that all he recognised was that they had force on their side: 'I know you have power enough.' Bradshaw did not know how to deal with this, nor the King's claim that he stood for the liberties of the people more than they did. 'Liberties', properly understood, of course, according to the laws, for it was not for the people to rule. Parliament no more stood for that than he did – for all they *said*. Radical spirits in the Army claimed that they were more representative of the people of England. That was not true either.

C.V. Wedgwood sums up: 'The progress of the trial was little short of disastrous. The leaders had been prepared for the King's refusal to recognise them. But they had not been prepared for his persistence in that refusal, nor for his claim to stand for the laws and liberties of his people – still less for his eloquence or for the authority of his presence and his words by which he dominated the proceedings.

'A judge of stronger personality and more experience than Bradshaw might have prevented him from doing so. But three times he had ordered the removal of the prisoner by the soldiers, because he could wring from him no admission whatever. On every occasion therefore he had drawn attention to precisely that element in the proceedings which should least have been emphasised – the overriding power of the Army, and the rule of force, not of law.'[1]

In his concluding speech Bradshaw recited the precedents for calling kings to account – Edward II and Richard II, though their misdeeds did not 'come near to the height and capitalness of crimes that are laid to your charge'. We see a touch of comedy in comparing Charles to Caligula. Or for that matter in calling upon him to repent his sins and implore the forgiveness of God for blood guiltiness, as David did for the death of Uriah. We are more struck by the offensiveness of this, from such people.

Even more so was the regular Puritan lie that the King had been responsible for the Massacre of

[1] C.V. Wedgwood, *A Coffin for King Charles*, 168.

Protestants in Ireland in 1641, and for hastening the death of his father, along with Buckingham. Milton twice repeated this shocking aspersion, when the only fault of those three had been that they were too fond of each other – if that were a fault.

Bradshaw was well rewarded for his performance, though the soldiery prevented anyone from hitting him over the head. He was paid £1000, and then awarded lands worth £2000 a year, which belonged to the Earl of St Albans and to Lord Cottington. When one notices how often the lands of the nobility were awarded to these lesser gentry, one cannot but think that there was an element of class envy at work – though it may be a piece of deplorable Marxism to notice it. The envy of middling people for aristocracy has been a continuing element in history – one notices it flagrantly in the French Revolution.

Bradshaw was made a member of the Commonwealth's Council of State, but was not popular there. The respectable Parliamentarian Whitelocke tells us that he was 'not much versed in such businesses, and spent much of their time by his own long speeches'. As Cromwell moved towards personal power – we must not blame him, for circumstances propelled him and the only practical thing to do was to take it on – Bradshaw moved into opposition. We must grant him the justice of his convictions. When Oliver sent the Long Parliament packing, not a town-cat mewed. But Bradshaw protested courageously: 'Sir, we have heard what you did in the House in the morning, and before many hours all England will hear it.' (All England didn't care.) 'Sir, you are mistaken to think the Parliament is dissolved, for no power under Heaven can dissolve them but themselves.'

For this he lost his Chief Justiceship of Chester, and the Lord Protector saw to it that Bradshaw was not returned to *his* Parliaments. The Protector did not like impracticable opposition any more than the King had done. When the great man died, the Rump did come back for a spell, and so did Bradshaw – to be thrown out by the Army, and back again. But it was too late for him, and for them all. Bradshaw's health was breaking down, and so was everything about them. The country wanted to get back to normality and the old known forms of government.

Bradshaw died on 31 October 1659, in time to avoid the jollifications of May 1660 – and a trial *he* would have encountered, if he had lived. Royalists execrated his memory. Buried in the Abbey, his body was exhumed at the Restoration and hung in chains at Tyburn along with Cromwell and Ireton, then reburied beneath the gallows.

The deanery at Westminster returned to its proper occupant.

John Cook, prosecutor at the 'Trial', took the place of the attorney-general. We must give him the credit of being a genuine law-reformer. He too was a Gray's Inn man, following upon Wadham College, Oxford. A Leicestershire man, he was well enough off when young to travel for some years on the Continent. In Geneva he stayed for months in the house of the theologian Diodati, father of the young man Milton was in love with – platonically, of course.

Returning, Cook went to Ireland, where Strafford employed him to revise the Irish Statutes. Later, he courageously paid tribute to Strafford's desire for law reform, when it was unpopular to defend him.

In the conflict between Army and Parliament Cook sided with the Army, surprisingly for a lawyer. He was a prolific pamphleteer, and justified the Army's occupation of the City upon 'its imprisonment of the best Christians for their consciences'. 'The best Christians' of course meant his own brand of Independents, disapproved of by disciplinary Presbyterians who meant to discipline them. The Army was 'bound by the law of God to deliver God's people and this whole kingdom from oppression both in souls and bodies'. In this case, the 'law of God' meant what Cook and his like fancied. One notices that in this period, as all through history, any argument serves to advance one's own interest or predilections. Cook's radical views were anathema to Presbyterians.

One night, going back to Gray's Inn, Cook was stopped by an acquaintance who said, 'I hear you are up to your ears in this business.' 'I am serving the people,' said Cook. 'There's a thousand to one will not give you thanks,' the man replied. We see how unpopular the whole affair was.

As prosecutor he took the Army officers' view that 'the King must die, and monarchy must die with him'. He even argued this in *An Appeal to All Rational Men!* This work appeared on the same day as *Eikon Basilike*, which portended to be a portrait of the King, his sufferings and prayers, by himself. In fact it was ghosted by a cleric, who was rewarded with a bishopric at the Restoration. For the book had a prodigious effect throughout the country, and was the foundation of the Anglican cult of King Charles the Martyr (he was a religious Anglican) for the next century. Milton answered it with his *Eikonoklastes*, which had no more effect than any other of his pamphlets.

Cook for his part compared the King to Cain, Machiavelli and Richard III. As for his own part in the 'Trial', 'I went cheerfully about it as to a wedding. And I hope it is meat and drink to good men to have justice done, and recreation to think what benefit the nation will receive by it.' He was rewarded by the mastership of St Cross Hospital at Winchester, subsequently forfeited when he went into opposition.

Cromwell had made him Chief Justice of Munster. Sailing from Wexford to Kinsale, he and his companions encountered an extreme storm, in which they nearly drowned (no doubt the Irish wished they had). This would have been a pity, for Cook proceeded to put into force the reforms on which he was so keen. 'He removed superfluous officers and reduced fees, abolished judges' fees and put them on straight salary, combined equity and common law practice, and held assize sessions in the country. He claimed to have decided 600 cases in two or three months; Cromwell remarked that Cook decided more cases in a week than Westminster Hall in a year. He also bent over backwards on behalf of the poor.' In England Cook actually pleaded that lawyers and physicians should remit every tenth fee to the poor. A novel amendment indeed to the tithes-system Cromwell dared not touch.

'He ridiculed the enthronement of precedent – "this over-doting upon old forms" – and the obfuscation of laws by antiquated language and procedure.' He favoured the use of English in law cases, in place of the Anglo-Norman gibberish which gave the profession a Trade Union monopoly. Mostly to no avail. The tide of reaction had already set in, and Cromwell, like a practical politician, had to go along with it – he agreed with it anyway. The conservative gentry of Cheshire did not want Bradshaw to represent them in Parliament. And Cook was left gesticulating in vain for reform. The traditional courts and procedures were restored and, like other adherents of the Good Old Cause, he had to protest to the Lord Protector.

Cook was an incorrigible republican, who was able to prove 'by Scripture and Reason that monarchical government is against the Mind of God, And that the execution of the late King was one of the fattest Sacrifices that ever Queen Justice had'. So he awaited his fate with confidence.

After three months in the Tower Cook was brought to trial at the Old Bailey on 14 October 1660. Nothing new transpired, except that somebody remembered the King nudging Cook with his cane to attract his attention to some point, and Cook taking no notice. Someone else remembered his fatal words that the King must die and monarchy with him. He admitted that he, Attorney-General Steele and Mr Aske had drawn up the charge, but argued that the words 'Tyrant, Traitor, Murderer' were not his, but those appointed to him. He raised various lawyerly points, such as that he could not be described in the specific words constituting treason according to the Statute, 25 Edward III.

Cook made an immensely long legalistic speech, and so did the Solicitor-General. Mr Wadham Wyndham rose to protest that the chief argument

that Cook sheltered himself under was his profession, 'which gives a blast to all of us of the long robe'.
We need not go into these tedious technicalities: the
facts were self-evident. In his last letter to his wife
he made a better defence, in rational terms – not the
delusions of the fanatics in resting all upon God's
will. He disclaimed being a fanatic and claimed only
the 'noble principle of preferring the universality,
before a particularity: which would have enfran-
chised the people, if the nation had not more
delighted in servitude than in freedom.'

Would it indeed? The answer to that rests upon a
correct reading of human psychology – whether men
in the mass are rational or no. An individual may be,
but the masses?

When his wife wept at saying farewell, he
consoled her with the words, 'Let us not part in a
shower. God hath wiped away all tears.'

We note the name of **Dr Dorislaus** in the
proceedings against the King. He was Dutch: what
was he doing there? The Army officers were out to
create maximum effect, and he was the only civil
lawyer they could get to take part. The son of a
minister in the Calvinist Dutch Church, he was
made a lecturer in civil law at Cambridge. His
lectures adumbrated the view that the people were
the source of monarchical power, and therefore had
the right to take up arms against an unjust
monarch. These lectures made a strong impression
on the young Milton. They would. It shows how right
Hobbes was about the deleterious influences upon
young people at the university – too young to know
what was sense, and what not.

101

Matthew Wren, the Laudian Master of Peterhouse, delated the lecturer to the Vice-Chancellor,
and got him to shut up. After a time he turned up
again, to inculcate – à propos of Tacitus – the study
of Roman law, and 'the examples of the histories'.
This was just what Hobbes deplored. Dorislaus was
the man for the revolutionaries, who called him in as
counsel to help draw up the charge against Charles
I. This incurred the bitter hatred of Royalists:
henceforward he was a marked man.

They had their chance when he was sent to
Holland, to prepare an alliance, and there they got
him. (So far from an alliance in a year or two the two
republics were at war.) In his native Holland
Dorislaus would take no notice of the warnings he
received. A party of Royalists, headed by a loyal
Scot, broke into the inn where he was staying, and
felled him, blow after blow, with 'Thus dies one of
the King's judges!'

John Downes was a barrister of Inner Temple, and
purchased the quasi-legal office of auditor of the
duchy of Cornwall. He had more business ability
than religious convictions, and so grew rich at the
expense of the Church. In 1643 he spoiled the bishop
of Chichester – Henry King, the cultivated poet – of
his corn and household provisions at Petworth, and
appropriated to himself two of the farms belonging
to the see, one of which he subsequently bought
outright. He followed this up by destroying the
bishop's palace in Chichester. When the lands of the
duchy of Cornwall were sold up by the triumphant
Commonwealth, Downes procured compensation of
£3,000. He was not a lawyer for nothing. For his

services on committees of the Army he was voted another £300.

At the King's trial he was the man who made a scene. Unsupported by religious convictions, he was humanly moved by the King's words. He rose to protest: 'Have we hearts of stone? Are we men?' He was held back by Cromwell's brother-in-law Walton, and Cawley. Cromwell himself turned on him: 'What ails thee? Art thou mad? Cans't thou not sit still and be quiet?' 'Sir, no – I cannot be quiet.' He tried to get up: 'If I die for it, I must do it.'

This helped him when his own turn came. He published a defence of himself as 'a weak, imprudent man ... ensnared through weakness and fear'. He pleaded that he was intimidated by Cromwell, truly enough. Indeed Cromwell had said, like the boss he was, 'Those that are gone in shall set their hands – I will have their hands now!' Hence, though condemned, he was reprieved from the death penalty and kept close prisoner in Newgate. Petitioning to Laud's nephew, Sir John Robinson, when lord mayor, Downes was moved into more comfortable quarters in the Tower, where he disappears from view.

Thomas, Lord Grey of Groby, had a bad press then and since. People thought of him as an apostate from his order, the nobility, son and heir of the earl of Stamford. Perhaps this goes to support my (Marxist) hunch as to class division; for the nobility, with some notorious exceptions, were with the King; it was the lesser gentry who supported Parliament, and provided a surprising number of Regicides.

Young Grey was not a bad fellow, but what we

103

should call a Leftist, indeed an extreme Leftist. He sided with the Army, fought spiritedly in the war, and then aided Pride's Purge, standing by the Colonel and pointing out fellow MPs who were to be excluded. In the High Court, as the only peer to take part in the proceedings, he was given precedence after Bradshaw, and had the dishonour of signing up immediately after the Lord President.

Subsequently he got out of step with the Lord Protector, who imprisoned him in Windsor Castle – then a convenient receptacle for such – on suspicion of being involved in Leveller plots against the government. What a disillusioning time Cromwell had altogether!

Shortly afterwards Lord Grey died, only thirty-five. If he had lived he would no doubt have made still more trouble for Charles II.

Henry Marten was another extreme Leftist, indeed an outspoken republican before anyone else, and was sent to the Tower by statesman Pym for uttering such untoward expressions, when the humbug of the early Long Parliament stated that they were fighting for 'King-and-Parliament'. Henry Marten was exceptional, for a politician, in having no humbug, in which Cromwell was a supreme master. I have hitherto done my best to do justice to Marten,[1] so here we may concentrate on him simply as Regicide.

An Oxford man, another from University College, he was another Gray's Inn man. In Parliament he was popular for his quips and jokes, something rare

[2] See my *Four Caroline Portraits*, ch. 3.

in that humourless assembly. It is to his credit that he spoke up against the imposition of the Scotch Covenant upon the English, by which – plus cash – Pym bought their alliance for the war. In spite of his republicanism he said, 'a king is but one master, and therefore likely to sit lighter upon our shoulders than a whole kingdom. And if he should grow so heavy as cannot well be borne, he may be sooner gotten off than they.' The Scottish alliance went forward: the English set little store by their silly Solemn Covenant.

At the crisis of the 'Trial' Marten took a serious hand. When the Army officers gathered in the Painted Chamber to plan the proceedings, the question arose by what authority they were to act. For a moment they were nonplussed, till Marten gave them their cue: 'In the name of the Commons in Parliament assembled, and all the good people of England.' When the Commonwealth required a new motto for their Great Seal, Marten supplied it: *Exit Tyrannus Regum ultimus*.

This was far from Charles I's conviction. He told Princess Elizabeth, in saying farewell to her, that his son would succeed him on the throne, and they would all be happier. The girl did not live to see it, she died in Carisbrooke Castle.

Marten had been so much to the fore in bringing down the King that it has always been a question how he avoided the death sentence. He was a good sort, and had several times helped to save the lives of Royalists (including reputedly, and not improbably, Shakespeare's Oxford by-blow, the dramatist Will Davenant). Marten – he preferred to be called Harry – was a gay cynic and an ardent woman-chaser. This was much disapproved of by the respectable Charles I; we cannot suppose that it was disapproved of by the cynical, unrespectable Charles II. Charles II was largely equipped for sport in bed; his strait-laced father was an under-sized man. These things are apt to determine people's 'principles'.

So Harry Marten got off the death penalty, and was confined, not too closely, at Chepstow Castle. He was allowed out occasionally to dine in the vicinity, where no doubt he was the soul of the party.

Thomas Scott became an intelligence man: he built up the spy service which was later so ably directed by Thurloe, and protected the Lord Protector from all the plots against him at home and abroad. Thurloe was so effective an operator that Charles II wanted to take him over into his service. Would that we had had him in our time, to uncover the Cambridge spies!

Scott was a Cambridge man (deplorable Emmanuel). He inherited money, and got more with his first wife. His second was the daughter of another Regicide, Mauleverer – by way of keeping it in the family. Scott was so convinced a republican that he opposed Cromwell as Protector, and helped to unseat his heir, Richard. He was so proud of his zeal as a Regicide that he wished to boast on his tomb, 'Here lies one who had a hand and a heart in the execution of Charles Stuart.' That settled his hash when his turn came. He died, still unrepentant, 'in a Cause not to be repented of '.

He had fled to Brussels, but was there recognised and persuaded to return and take his chance. No indemnity or oblivion for him. He was a purchaser of Church lands, and one of those who took over Lambeth Palace. Here he helped to wreck the chapel, destroyed Archbishop Parker's monument and threw out his bones upon the rubbish heap. He deserved his fate for that alone.

The Parliamentary visitors thrust his son into a fellowship at All Souls. But he continued his father's trade by spying for Charles II, being recruited into the service by his engaging mistress, Aphra Behn, novelist, dramatist, and feminist.

Adrian Scrope must have been a descendant of the medieval family who had an intriguing Archbishop-martyr (of York) in it. Yet another Oxford man, he was of Hart Hall and Middle Temple. He married a Waller, his mother-in-law an aunt of John Hampden – so how could he escape that popular cult? Scrope scrupulously attended all but one of the sessions of the High Court, and signed the death warrant. When his regiment mutinied against service in Ireland, Cromwell and Fairfax put paid to them.

Scrope was made governor of Bristol Castle; when it was ordered to be demolished, he was compensated with a well-paid job in Scotland. It is again a revealing character as to class prejudice that the new régime destroyed or 'slighted' so many castles that harboured the nobility – Raglan or Montgomery or Ashby-de-la-Zouch, for instance. One still sees the toppling towers.

At the Restoration Scrope surrendered himself to the proclamation. The House of Commons voted to include him under the Act of Indemnity, with a heavy fine, and for a time he was set free on parole.

The House of Lords refused to allow him to be pardoned. It is noticeable that the Lords were more severe – perhaps not only because many of the Commons had had a poor record. At his trial Scrope did not fail to point to the record of some of those who now sat in judgment on him.

It was not that, however, that did him in. A former colleague, Richard Browne, who had been a major-general in the Army, betrayed Scrope's private confidence. Even after Charles II's return Scrope had unwisely justified Charles I's execution to Browne. Scrope concluded that it was this betrayal that did for him. He had a grandson who was out in Monmouth's rebellion. Monmouth spent his last night before Sedgemoor in the Scrope family house in Somerset, lovely Brympton D'Evercy. There I have seen before now a touching portrait of Monmouth's body after his execution – unwise young bastard of Charles II, and his favourite.

Sir John Bourchier was the grandson and heir, as a child, of a Yorkshire knight, for his father died insane – so what could one expect? He grew up to be of a violent, quarrelsome temper. He was made to make humble submission to the House of Lords for contesting a judgment of the Lord Keeper. He then quarrelled with his neighbour Wentworth over forest rights in the Forest of Galtre. For breaking down fences he was fined and imprisoned. He next had a dispute with Lord Savile about petitions to Parliament.

Yorkshire was his stamping ground, and he stamped away promoting Puritanism there to good (or bad) effect. He received his reward by being worked into the Long Parliament as a recruiter member for Ripon. This built up Puritan membership, though Bourchier was an Independent. Recruited also to the High Court he rarely attended, but signed the death-warrant.

By the time of the Restoration he was moribund himself, and so was allowed to face his end in the care of his daughter. Urged to recant, he forced himself upright and spat out, 'I tell you it was a good act, and God and good men will own it.' And thereupon gave up the ghost, to receive his proper reward hereafter.

CHAPTER 7

Londoners

Why should **John Milton** escape being regarded as a regicide, as he escaped the penalties too? He was the foremost defender of the crime – before all Europe – the most frequent and the most voluminous, in tract after tract. How did he come to escape punishment? That has always remained a question. He was lucky.

He was very much a Londoner, his father a well-to-do scrivener, his mother daughter of a merchant tailor. All distinctly middle-class. Educated at St Paul's, he was much influenced by an inveterately Puritan master, one Gill. This unfortunate influence was confirmed when he went up to Cambridge, for Christ's College was second only to Emmanuel for Puritanism.

After some cultivated years in Italy, he returned home: 'I thought it base that I should travel abroad for the cultivation of my mind while my fellow-citizens at home were fighting for liberty.' 'Liberty'? – they got military dictatorship, and Milton served it well. However, he did not fight. 'As his mind had always been stronger than his body, he did not court camps in which any common person would have been as useful as himself.' Always superior, always supercilious, he regarded his own Commonwealth Council of State as consisting of 'mechanics, soldiers, servants, strong and keen enough but entirely ignorant of public political matters'.

This was quite unfair – he never had any conception of fairness: they understood politics better than he did. He was a doctrinaire intellectual.

He fought with his pen, tirelessly, whether anybody took him seriously, or no – mostly not. Christopher Hill described him as 'a profoundly *political* animal'. This is a typical misjudgment. Milton had no conception of the normal exigencies, the necessary compromises, of politics. He was an idealist – and a colossal egoist, who thought he could tell everybody what was right and what to do. About married life too, where he was notoriously unsuccessful. When he quoted the Bible's authority for polygamy, his fellow Puritans – comic to think – accused him of that shocking deviation. He did not recognise any equality between men and women in regard to divorce; women were inferior (the Puritan view). But the Bible disapproved of divorce – its authority was good, except when it did not agree with John Milton.

He and his father owed a debt to the Church – the father had been a chorister at Christ Church, Oxford. No matter, the son took up pen against 'the obscene and surfeited priest', and 'the ignoble huckstering of piddling tithes'. Later he became disillusioned of his hopes from Presbyterians and, finding that 'presbyter was but priest writ large', attacked them. He became disillusioned with everybody, except himself and the heterodox Sir Henry Vane. *Paradise Lost* is an epic of disillusionment.

He was the first person to defend the Regicides,

rushing into print with his *Tenure of Kings and Magistrates* a fortnight after the appalling crime. He did not rest his defence upon popular sovereignty – the people never had any good words from him – but upon some 'freedom' in accord with God's will. Nor did any question of the High Court's legality bother him: he asserted that 'in whose hand soever is found sufficient power to avenge tyranny is self-evidently entitled to do so'. That is, force is all. One sees that this asserter of 'liberty', this defender of 'freedom', would have no difficulty in going along with Cromwell's military dictatorship. The poor King had been right in regarding himself as a better expositor of the people's liberties, rightly understood.

What was true about Milton was, not that he was 'profoundly political', but that he was profoundly ambitious. A little man, he was bent on stretching himself in every direction – in literature as in public life. Imagine writing *Paradise Lost*, when blind, attempting something 'never attempted yet' by any other hand! It was wonderful of him.

He got his footing in public life as Secretary for Foreign Tongues for the Commonwealth, and thereupon was given the job of answering the King's book, *Eikon Basilike*, which, as we saw, he did very offensively with his *Eikonoklastes*. When the much respected foreign scholar, Saumaise, put forward his Defence of the King, Milton replied in still more vituperative Latin. Hobbes commented that it is hardly to be judged which is the best Latin or which is the worst reasoning. He thought them both rhetorical exercises – like disputations in the schools – *ex parte*, of course.

For the Lord Protector Milton produced yet

another, *Defensio Secunda*, and his Latin tracts won him at last fame on the Continent. When foreigners came to London they wanted to see the notorious author. When the Republic was breaking up, Milton rushed forward with tract upon tract, signalling frantically like a stranded sailor on the sea-coast of Patagonia. He was indeed stranded, helpless and hopeless. Nobody took any notice. There are tides in politics, as Michael Oakeshott instructs us, which are inevitable and one can do nothing about it.

All that Milton could do was to go into hiding and lie low until the worst of the storm was over. The Restoration Parliament ordered all copies of his *Defensio* to be burnt by the common hangman. That summer he was arrested, then released on payment of his prison fees. Obstinate as ever, he protested that they were excessive.

It was very civilised of Clarendon to keep Milton's name off the list of those to be pursued, a mere stroke of the pen would have done. Various people did their best to get him off – members of the literary confraternity mainly. Andrew Marvell, whom Milton had got into the Commonwealth secretariat, now got up a party for him in the Commons. Milton had helped Davenant in his time of danger; now Davenant turned to and exerted himself for Milton. If Davenant was, as he liked to think, Shakespeare's son, how appropriate, for we know how much the younger, more attractive Milton admired the dramatist. Now, such are life's little ironies, the family at Stratford-on-Avon were Royalists.

Isaac Penington was an acquaintance of Milton in the City. As a fishmonger he became alderman and sheriff; when Parliament pushed out the Lord Mayor for being a Royalist, Penington was thrust in in his place. The King never recognised this illegal intrusion. But Penington was very holy. It fell to him to destroy the communion rails in the City churches, and he was so sabbatarian as to order no sale of milk on Sundays after 8 a.m. in summer, and 9 a.m. in winter. For his services and qualities, the Speaker of the Commons, usurping the King's prerogative, knighted him. Need we recognise it?

His greatest services were in raising cash and loans in the City for Parliament. Thus Pym was enabled to retain the Scottish Army in the North to pressure the King, even before the war. For this and one thing and another Penington got grants of land outside London, and houses and tenements in the City belonging to the bishop, or to the see of Winchester. It was he who conducted poor old Archbishop Laud up to the scaffold in 1645.

At his own trial he made a rather pitiable figure, pleading 'ignorance of what he did' at the King's trial. So, let off the death penalty, he was confined in the Tower, where he died at the end of that happy year.

Owen Rowe was apprenticed as a haberdasher, became a liveryman, silk merchant and a member of the Common Council. With Penington he was a leading member of the congregation of St Stephen's, Coleman Street, that favourite receptacle of Puritans, where he was on the committee to select only worthy communicants. He had a share in the Massachusetts Bay Company and bought property intending to settle there. He also had interests in

the Bermuda Company, and at one time sold 700 lb
of the noxious weed, tobacco, in London. It was the
Puritans who were the imperialists (in the Marxist
sense).

As a lieutenant-colonel in charge of the City's
arms and ammunition magazine at the Tower he
became the central administrator of arms for
Parliament. As such he supplied arms for thousands
of troops all over the country. (What a waste!) He
proved a most efficient organiser, and his strict
convictions prevented him from taking the opportunities this presented for embezzlement or even
jiggery-pokery. No complaints made. In fact he
found himself in debt for his devoted service. An
appointment to run the Militia of London, with
friend Penington, came in handy, and later he got a
job in the Customs.

A trustee for the sale of lands belonging to Deans
and Chapters, with his fellow Regicide, Tichborne,
Rowe opposed Cromwell's order for settling some of
these. Two other Regicides, Jones and Corbet, tried
to persuade the Protector to honour Parliament's
grant of lands in Ireland in satisfaction of the large
public debt to Rowe. Imperialist Puritans regarded
Ireland as a colony, along with others.

At the Restoration Rowe was an old man, and was
spared the death penalty. He died in the Tower –
familiar surroundings to him, it must have seemed
like home – the very next year. Rowe's brother
married the daughter of the Regicide Scott. One sees
how closely knitted together these people were,
beliefs and all.

Robert Tichborne was originally a draper, but

when young found it more exciting to join the army (who wouldn't?). He rapidly became a captain. Then, when there was a likelihood of the Presbyterian Parliament gaining control of the City, the Army saw Parliament off with a speedily raised regiment, of which Tichborne was made colonel. He was an Independent, a Radical sympathetic to some Leveller demands, without going the whole hog with them. He was practical man enough to realise that tithes could not be abolished without social disruption, and were indispensable to any national organisation of religion.

That practical man Oliver Cromwell realised this full well, and his brother-in-law, Wilkins, Warden of Wadham, warned him that religion in England could not be run without bishops either. When the Lord Protector took on the royal prerogative of knighting such people as Tichborne, and setting up his own House of Lords, one wonders that he didn't go in for touching for the King's Evil too, so popularly practised by the saintly Charles II.

Tichborne was a bit of a Saint, too, and wrote two devotional works, *A Cluster of Canaan's Grapes* and *The Rest of Faith*. They are said to be full of emotional piety. I have not read these uplifting works. The Lord Protector sacked him from his job as a Customs Commissioner, but 'whether because of non-payment of large arrears to the Exchequer or misappropriation concerning smuggled gold bars is uncertain'.

His piety was no help to him at his trial; his plea of youth in 1649 may have been of more avail. For, in spite of being 'one of the most aggressive and persistent of the Regicides both in and out of the

High Court', he was not awarded death. He was imprisoned for the rest of his life, and lost the 'considerable lands and goods he had acquired'.

Sir John Danvers offers a refreshing contrast – he was an aristocratic playboy. He belonged to a family that had already seen much trouble. An older brother had killed the heir to the Long family, in a bitter family feud (it sparked off *Romeo and Juliet*).[1] This brother, Henry Danvers, was the boy-friend of young Southampton, who was not platonic – and Henry never married, but built up a large fortune instead. He also gave the Botanical Garden to the university of Oxford. The youngest brother was such a spendthrift that Henry would never leave him his fortune. The oldest brother, Sir Charles, had been executed for his part in Essex's rebellion.

Aubrey knew the family well, and tells us that young John 'travelled France and Italy, and made good observations. He had in a fair body an harmonical mind. In his youth his complexion was so exceeding beautiful and fine ... that his companion in his travels did say that the people would come after him in the street to admire him.' No doubt in Italy ... compare the attraction that the beautiful, but uncompromising, young Milton, 'the lady of Christ's', exercised upon inflammable Italians.

Oddly enough Sir John married the well-known Lady Magdalen Herbert, who was twice his age with ten children; however, she was a rich widow with a castle in Wales. She was the patron of Donne, who

[1] See my *Shakespeare the Man*, 108–9.

tells us that, with Danvers' looks and expectations, he could have married anybody he fancied. For a second wife he married another heiress, who brought him an estate in Wiltshire. He bought himself a fine house in Chelsea, which he furnished sumptuously, and where he created a famous garden. ' 'Twas Sir John Danvers of Chelsea,' Aubrey writes, 'who first taught us that way of Italian gardens'. He created another splendid garden at his wife's place, Lavington.

Much may be forgiven him for this, but of course he spent himself out, and was always in debt. Though a gentleman of Charles I's privy chamber, he would not contribute to the King's expedition against the Covenanting Scots, and passed over into outright opposition. Brother Henry, a saving man, left all his estate to their sister, nothing to extravagant John. People said that it was the pressure of debt that made him go in with Parliament, and then go on with Cromwell. Clarendon called him 'a proud formal man. Between being seduced and a seducer, he became so far involved in their counsels that he suffered himself to be applied to their worst offices.' This meant taking part regularly in the sessions of the High Court, and signing up.

He luckily died in the first year of the Protectorate, in April 1655, or his misdeed would have caught up with him in 1660.

John Venn was a Merchant Taylor, who rose from apprenticeship to be Warden of the Company. He was a regular attendant at All Hallows, Bread Street – the street in which Milton was born – a church which was a hot-bed of Puritanism, if not of the purity of its clergy. Very thick with the young apprentices out for mischief, he mobilised them into mobs, like the one he led down to Whitehall to terrorise the King into consenting to Strafford's execution. This lay badly upon Charles's conscience for ever after.

Venn regularly took a dirty hand in organising the petitions sent down from the City, for they were cooked and contained far more signatures than had actually been signed. Cornelius Burgess, the popular preacher who made money out of it, was another expert at this game.[2] More creditably, Venn was a founding member of the Massachusetts Bay Company. Less so, he was instrumental in getting the Common Council under Radical control.

A member of many Parliamentary committees, he took advantage of that for the sale of the Bishops' lands to acquire some for himself. Again as Governor of Windsor Castle he was said to have made gains from its plunder and pillage. There was plenty there.[3] Still, Parliament voted him £4000 to defray expenses for the destruction he wrought – Charles I, like the aesthete he was, had made it and St George's Chapel into a veritable treasure-house. Charles II had to rebuild a great deal of the upper quadrangle where the Royal apartments were. One must remember, however, in regard to these large grants made by Parliament to those who served its purposes, that it is doubtful whether the full amounts reached them, or even were expected to. There was an element of the notional about such things.

[2] For him see my *Reflections on the Puritan Revolution*, 14-15, 31.
[3] See *ibid.*, 42–3, 112–13.

Venn was much influenced by the prominent Presbyterian preacher, Christopher Love, who became chaplain of his regiment, after being expelled from Oxford. In a few years Venn fell out of love with Love, though he is thought to have remained a Presbyterian. This was unusual for one of the judges in 1649. Venn died the next year, luckily for him.

Augustine Garland was the son of a prosperous London attorney, but was on bad terms with his father and also the rest of the family, who came off better in the parental will in consequence. A pensioner of Emmanuel College, Cambridge, he went on to Lincoln's Inn, where he distinguished himself by leading a student riot. This was on behalf of some punishment awarded to Nicholas Love, to be found as colleague again as Regicide. Evidently birds of a feather, trouble-makers.

Garland was an even more attentive member of Parliamentary committees than Venn – constantly used to do their dirty work. 'The report shall be made by Mr Garland' was the continual refrain. It fell to him to report to Parliament – the small Rump that was left of it after the Purge of the majority – the ordinance constituting the High Court, drafting and reporting the amendments to and fro, which took him all one night. How expeditiously they worked at their mischief!

It seems that Garland's convictions were republican. Then why did he propose to Parliament that Cromwell should be crowned king? – enthusiastically seconded by Henry Cromwell of course. It is thought that Garland's motive was to regularise and legitimise the military dictatorship. This was Oliver's hope too – as if anything could!

At his own trial Garland pleaded that he had signed the death warrant 'for fear of my own destruction. I did not know which way to be safe in anything.' He denied that he had spat at the King. Someone had spat near, but not at, him. (Seventeenth-century hygiene!) He got off the death sentence, and was transported to Tangier, which had come to England as part of the dowry of Charles II's wife. There Garland disappears from our view. He is unlikely ever to have come home again to the scenes where he had been, lamentably, so active.

CHAPTER 8

Locals and Localities

It is in the country that we see best the reaction to these revolutionary events at the centre. When we say 'country' we meant the conscious, leading elements of society, who ruled it, for the people at large were the objects of rule, not rulers. These were essentially the gentry, who ruled their counties as Justices of the Peace, from Quarter Sessions, a county gathering, through lesser offices and administrators, vestries, constables and such, in the parishes where the squires kept such order as could be in the nursery.

In the counties we see most clearly the class-configuration behind events, and which ultimately decided them. It is not too much to say that the country at large was affronted by the Revolution at the centre, and went into sullen opposition. The country clearly reacted against the Puritan revolutionaries, who kept a tight grip on affairs through their too conspicuous instrument, the Army. It became obvious what difficulty the Revolution had to find respectable people to carry on local administration.

For now both sections of the governing class, who

had fought each other in the Civil War, were in opposition to the Puritan government, by force, of the three kingdoms. It was a thoroughly unnatural state of affairs – England could not for long be governed against its 'natural rulers', the whole balance of social forces. At any rate, not for long – only as long as the Army remained united under its grandee leader (a great politician, even statesman), upon whose death the whole nation revolted against military rule.

Now, both the Royalist *and* Parliamentarian sections of the governing class were in opposition. This shows up in every county. Take a representative county like Sussex, for example – all the more representative because it had been divided.[1]

West Sussex was mainly Royalist, with a concentration in and around its cathedral city, Chichester. The gentry of East Sussex were dominantly Parliamentarian, under the lead of their local magnate, Sir Thomas Pelham. He now went into taciturn, but entire, opposition to the new unwelcome régime, taking his following with him. Eleven members of the Commission of the Peace went out of it, their places as JPs taken by lesser men. Some of the gentry – Parliament men, moderates – remained as JPs, but would have nothing to do with the Army, with a régime that was 'blatantly military with its patrolling troops'. Even a couple among the county's Regicides withdrew – Downes and Cawley; while the most inveterate of them, Anthony Stapley, attended affairs at the centre only fitfully and, before the end, was ready to

[1] Cf. Anthony Fletcher, *A County Community in Peace and War, Sussex 1600–1660*, from which quotations are taken.

recognise the inevitable return of the old order.

Cromwell himself longed to return to constitutional forms – this was the real reason for his wish to revive kingship in himself, not just personal ambition, as everybody said. (He was well qualified for it, except that he hadn't the qualification.) He found Sussex 'an intransigent county', like so many others. The county, i.e. its gentry, opposed his nominations for his parliaments; nor could he get agreement from these, even when his second parliament had a hundred members excluded from it for the purpose. A Rye gentleman declared comprehensively, 'None but rogues fought against the King – Cromwell and all that followed him were rogues.' This was rather too comprehensive, positively unfair.

Such was the background of opposition in the counties that induced Cromwell to try the experiment of governing them through his Major-Generals.

Sussex fell into the group of counties consigned to the care of the Regicide **Goff**. His only qualifications were his dedication to his Puritan nonsense, even more his personal attachment to the charismatic Cromwell. He prayed for the Protector 'without ceasing', he reported, but was shocked to find that many 'sought to render his Highness unto the people of God as a person void of religion or the power of Godliness'. This was shocking indeed, after all the evidences. Goff had been inspired by millenarian hopes, or illusions, earlier. Even now 'God can yet raise that design out of the dust, and make it turn to His praise, and the comfort of those that love the Lord Jesus Christ, and wait for the rise of

Antichrist'. Some hopes!

Only a few of the lesser gentry attended the Major-General's call. After meeting them, 'I do see the stress of this business must lie upon the middle sort of men'. The business of decimating Royalist delinquents to finance Cromwell's government was not at all to the minds of the gentry: they dragged their feet and would not cooperate in a task that offended against the neighbourliness and common class-interest. 'The gentry community was bound to close its ranks against him.'

Major-General Goff grew discouraged. He confessed himself 'so much tired that I can scarce give an account of my doings'; moreover 'most of the commissioners are tired and desired to be dismissed for the present'. The experiment had to be given up: 'the maintenance of the Major-Generals and their subordinates had been sabotaged by the gentry.' Cromwell was thrown back upon another attempt at a parliament of his calling. With no better hope.

The gentry were coming together again, reconciliation was in the air – or, we may say, they were learning their lesson from adversity. Even so notorious a Royalist as John Ashburnham, so conspicuous from his personal attendance upon Charles I to the end, had his estate reduced from £850 to £200, somewhat mysteriously, for claims upon it. Even the Regicide Stapley was prepared to listen to the persuasions of his Royalist kin that the return of Charles II was desirable, and not only feasible but necessary to avoid anarchy.

A Sussex gent wrote that during this distressful decade offices were filled up by a kind of 'pitiful creature as were never heard of till these times'.

This was perhaps too dismissive, but he had a point. At the other end of the south coast, Colonel Bennett ran Cornwall for Cromwell. He was a gent, just, but indeed had been never heard of till these times. The chief Parliamentarian magnate, Lord Robartes (a *nouveau riche* peer), had gone into opposition as much as the loyal Royalists.

Now they were all coming together. 'The Sussex gentry, like those of Kent, enthusiastically welcomed the Restoration.' Only a few Puritan militants (we might readdress the term 'malignants' to them now) and Regicides were absent from the county's address of welcome to the returned King.

Who were these last, socially speaking?

We learn that 'Stapley was the only Regicide with an impeccable county background, Cawley was hardly established in county society, James Temple was the careerist son of a recently settled family, Downes's background remains bafflingly obscure, and Norton was clearly an upstart.'

They had done well for themselves while the sun shone on them. 'Stapley and Norton were purchasers of Church lands.' Downes, who had proved so reluctant at Charles I's Trial, until Cromwell ordered him into line, acquired most of the Close at Chichester, demolished the Chancellor's house, and made himself comfortable in the Deanery. But not for long.

Anthony Stapley had been at Cambridge and Gray's Inn. At Lewes he took part in setting up one of those Puritan lectureships which set Archbishop Laud at defiance. He prevailed on his fellow JPs to resist Laud's order for putting communion tables at the east end of chancels. This 'ungodly innovation', as Puritans called it, was – apart from anything else – a question of seemliness. In the open chancel the table was ready to hand for people to put hats and coats on, exposed also to the attentions of their dogs.

Stapley had appointed as chaplain to his regiment the 'eminent Puritan divine', Francis Cheynell.[2] This was the odious man who persecuted the dying Chillingworth, brought out from the siege of Arundel Castle.

Stapley's colleague in doing ill in Sussex was **James Temple**, a kinsman of Leicestershire's disgrace, Peter Temple. Head of the clan was Sir Peter Temple who, though nominated for the High Court, refused to sit. James Temple was nephew to the impossible Lord Say and Sele. Busy-body Cheynell reported that Temple's defence of Bramber Castle was 'the wonder of all the country' – a plaque records it on the ruins. As a member of the Committee for Sequestrations Temple made himself comfortable at Michelgrove, the Royalist Shelleys' estate. With his close friend and colleague, Challoner, he was sent to serve in Ireland.

At the Restoration he attempted to flee there, but was intercepted at Coventry, and sent to the Tower. At his own trial he pleaded that he had been duped into sitting at the King's, and that he had signed the death warrant under duress. This may have been true, so he was let off with life imprisonment, and sent to join the jolly party in Jersey.

His immediate family connections were impeccably Calvinist. A daughter married Admiral Corne-

---

[2] For him see my *Reflections on the Puritan Revolution*, 83, 158.

lius Van Tromp, while Temple's second wife was a daughter of Admiral Martin Van Tromp.

Sir Gregory Norton, though active in Sussex, was born in Berkshire. His family had been involved in Irish affairs in Elizabeth I's reign. Hence his Irish baronetcy. Norton was an intimate friend of Humphry Edwards, and even more adept at making away with Crown and Royalist properties. He was recruited to the Rump along with his fellow Regicide, Cawley, with whom he co-ordinated his activities. For these Norton was rewarded with a grant of £1000 and Sir Roger Palmer's confiscated house at Charing Cross. The money did not materialise, so Norton conveniently discovered that the Royalist Sir Henry Hastings, in compounding for his 'delinquency', had sensibly concealed what he could.

After dancing attendance on the High Court regularly and signing the death warrant, Norton got the grant of Richmond Palace, along with much of its furniture. From Royalist confiscations Norton took more than he was owed for his nefarious services. Thus, after his death, his widow had to pay back the overplus of £516 he had made.

In Nottinghamshire peers and gentry were mainly Royalist, but the county was won for Parliament by the energy and tenacity of **Colonel John Hutchinson** of Owthorpe. He held on to the strategically decisive position of Nottingham Castle throughout a long siege. After the destruction of the war the Castle had to be rebuilt – and was, as a Renaissance palace, by the returned Marquis of Newcastle, one of

Bess of Hardwick's remarkable progeny.

Hutchinson was upheld by his unquestioned Puritan convictions, shared equally by his wife, an insufferable snob. Hutchinson was a Peterhouse man at Cambridge, though its High Church flavouring did him no good. His wife, in her biography of him, wrote enthusiastically of his piety. He inclined to Independency, i.e. Congregationalism, but under the stress of the siege received an illumination against infant baptism, and that adult Baptism was the right thing. I do not know whether he was a General or a Particular Baptist, in any case not a religion for a gentleman – as Charles II said of Presbyterianism.

During the prolonged siege Hutchinson received handsome offers from his cousins, the Royalist Byrons, if only he would surrender. These were religiously refused: God was with him, and he was above such carnal things. His service was of the greatest value to the Good Cause – not yet Old – for Nottingham was of crucial strategic value in the Midlands.

An extreme believer, he signed the protest against Parliament's agreeing to the concessions made to the King at the last moment in their Treaty of Newport. He followed this up by consenting to become one of the King's judges. Later on, his wife said that he was nominated against his will; but, 'looking upon himself as called hereunto, durst not refuse it, as holding himself obliged by the covenant of God'. She said that it was only after long prayer and inward wrestling that he signed the death warrant. I dare say.

According to his wife, Hutchinson 'infinitely

disliked the action of the Army'[3] in its Purge of Parliament – though he took part in its criminal proceedings all the same. Thereafter he distrusted Oliver Cromwell, thinking him motivated by carnal ambition, though we know that it was God's Providence that moved him. (However, this mistrust and subsequent opposition helped him when his own trial came.) Meanwhile, his cousin Ireton got him on to the Commonwealth Council of State.

When things caught up with him, he pleaded sincere repentance, confessing his involvement in 'so horrid a crime as merits no indulgence'. His petition for mercy arose, he said, from 'a thorough conviction of his former misled judgment and conscience', and he was pleading not out of regard for his own safety.

Rather shockingly, he was let off completely. The greatest exertions were made on his behalf by his wife's Royalist relations, and by the Byrons. His wife says that 'he was not very well satisfied in himself for accepting the deliverance. While he saw others suffer, he suffered with them in his mind; and, had not his wife persuaded him, offered himself a voluntary sacrifice.' That would seem a work of supererogation. She 'thought she had never deserved so well of her husband as in the endeavours and labours she exercised to bring him off, but found she had never displeased him more in her life, and much ado to persuade him to be content with his deliverance'. That may be as it may be.

The government cannot have been best pleased, for they kept a wary eye upon him. Three years later they arrested him on suspicion of being concerned in

---

[3] A.C. Wood, *Nottinghamshire in the Civil War*, 157.

a plot in neighbouring Yorkshire. He was finally imprisoned in ruinous, insalubrious Sandown Castle. This salved his conscience: he regarded it as freeing him from any obligations to the government and refused to give any engagement for future behaviour to purchase release. He even printed a narrative of the hard usage he had received in the Tower from Sir John Robinson, Archbishop Laud's nephew. If so, nothing like what poor Laud suffered.

Hutchinson, a cultivated gentleman, had purchased some of the King's pictures at the Commonwealth's sales of them. Charles I's collection had been about the finest in Europe, outside the Vatican. He had purchased the whole Gonzaga collection from Mantua at one swoop. The Philistine Commonwealth dispersed most of it. One sees the Titians that were at Whitehall in the Louvre, and the Mantegnas in the Prado. This is where Charles I's heart was, rather than in politics. (Who can blame him? Michael Oakeshott, professor of the subject, thought it a second-rate activity.)

At any rate Charles II got back his father's pictures from Hutchinson. The Sidney family at Penshurst, who had gone in with Cromwell, returned theirs.

Lucy Hutchinson was at Owthorpe when the Colonel died in 1664. 'Let her, as she is always above other women, show herself in this occasion a good Christian, and above the pitch of ordinary women.' She thought herself so too. 'My father and mother, fancying me beautiful, and more than ordinarily apprehensive [intelligent] spared no cost to improve me in my education.' She then goes into it in detail. She even translated the unbelieving Lucretius. As she waxed more Puritan and Baptismal, she became ashamed of it, and regarded 'the study of pagan poets and philosophers as one great means of debauching the learned world'.

The Hutchinsons were an obstinate, self-righteous, stuck-up couple.

A lesser Notts renegade was **Thomas Millington** of Felley abbey, a family roosting on monastic property. Perhaps this gave him a further propulsion as to the way he should go – the Puritans all wished to carry the Reformation further, and get their hands on more Church lands. Mrs Hutchinson said, in her pleasant way, that Millington was two-faced and an evil liver. This did not disqualify him from running the county's committee to eject 'scandalous', i.e. loyal, ministers; as Clerk and a lawyer he made the most of his opportunities.

Like Hutchinson he was a Peterhouse man, but does not appear to have shared his religious enthusiasm. At his own trial Millington pleaded that he had been carried along by fear and awe of the Army in power.

He himself seems not to have fought, but concentrated on his county committee. His legal qualification indicated him for the High Court. Years later his own sentence was commuted to life imprisonment. Already elderly, in his sixties, he spent his remaining years in the salubrious isle of Jersey.

Robert Lilburne the Regicide was the elder brother of 'Honest John', 'Freeborn Lilburne', the irrepressible agitator and Leveller pamphleteer, author of some eighty pamphlets, nearly all of them self-advertising, Sir Charles Firth tells us. I could not bear to read them. Though he was often shut up in prison, nothing would ever shut him up. He had an insatiable itch to be in the public eye and the public prints. A public nuisance. He gave Oliver Cromwell a great deal of trouble, who treated him at first with much patience – i.e. while he needed to – but before the end his patience ran out.

The Regicide brother was a more serious person, though a Baptist – he could not abide the Presbyterians with their discipline and inflated view of themselves. As commander-in-chief in Scotland he dissolved the General Assembly of the Kirk. This must have given pleasure to many. He shared the Army point of view, and had a hand in the *Declaration of the English Army in Scotland*, which called on Cromwell 'to set up the kingdom of Jesus Christ' in England. Oliver did what he could.

Parliament voted Lilburne lands worth £300 a year for services in Scotland, while his salaries there amounted to over £1000 a year. However, neither Parliament nor Protector pleased him long. He opposed making Oliver king, and was held to be a malcontent. Of Parliament he 'hoped never a true Englishman would name the Parliament again, and he would have the House pulled down where they sat, for fear it should be infectious'.

Perhaps malcontentment was in the Lilburnes' Durham blood. They were outrageously North Country. John Lilburne died before the popular Restoration took place to annoy him, and was buried appropriately in the churchyard adjoining Bedlam. Robert petitioned for pardon both before and after his trial, at which he confessed his sense of guilt, pleaded that he had acted ignorantly, and would have saved the King's life if he could. This saved his own, and he got imprisonment for life on St Nicholas Island in Plymouth Sound. Today we call it Drake's Island.

John Blakiston was another North Country pusher. He belonged to a family which had been Catholic Recusants – anything to be out of step. His father was out of step as a High Church Laudian prebendary of Durham cathedral, and that was very unpopular. John must have reacted against father Marmaduke, for he became a violent Puritan, no less obstreperous.

The son married a well-to-do Newcastle widow, and this provided a useful foundation for his rising local career. Becoming alderman, then mayor, he arrived MP for Newcastle, after a disputed election. In Parliament his main interest was in religious issues, and it must have given him pleasure to take part in squashing the Church courts. He was also useful in extending Parliamentary control in the North, getting leave of absence to keep Newcastle in line. Becoming increasingly Radical, he was so hostile to the Bishops (he evidently had a complex), that people thought him an Anabaptist. This shocking aspersion was like being called a Bolshevik in the 1920s. Perhaps he deserved it, being behind the Newcastle petition against accommodation with the King.

He was no less active in the baleful proceedings of January 1649, attending every session and signing the death warrant. His own death warrant came shortly after, unexpectedly, for he was only in his forties. He was related by marriage to another North Country Regicide, Sir John Bourchier.

We learn that 'the latter part of his Parliamentary career was clouded by accusations of corruption and of interference on behalf of his numerous delinquent relatives'. If so, that may be counted in his favour – rather human.

Since Yorkshire was the largest of counties, it produced a fair number of Regicides, four in all. **John Alured**, or Aldred, married a cousin of Peregrine Pelham, another Yorkshire Regicide. He was converted to godliness by contact, purely verbal, with the Emmanuelite, Shepherd, who was convinced of the wickedness of the sign of the cross, kneeling and the surplice. Though elected to Parliament Alured played no part in it, but concentrated on local work, especially disarming Recusant Catholics, of whom Yorkshire had not a few. He seems to have known Andrew Marvell, son of the vicar of Winestead near Hull, and may have helped him.

Alured, or Aldred, died before his crime in attending the High Court could be brought home to him. He was attainted all the same, and his possessions confiscated.

Sir William Constable of Flamborough was a grander figure, who purchased a baronetcy from James I and married a daughter of the first Lord Fairfax. Though religiously a Puritan, he lived extravagantly and was always in debt. This forced him to sell his family estate to Sir Marmaduke

Langdale, who took the Royalist side later. The war enabled Constable to recover the estate on account of Langdale's 'delinquency' – Parliamentary semantics for being on the other side. Chronically in debt in the 1630s Constable thought of emigrating to America, but spent four years in Holland to avoid creditors. The troubles in England gave him a chance to rehabilitate himself, and he fought alongside the Fairfaxes all over the East Riding with great success. His nephew, the second Lord Fairfax, procured £1900 from Parliament to compensate his old uncle.

Over the trial and execution of the King, Constable actively supported Cromwell, not Fairfax. So he was given an elaborate – shall we say, propagandist – state funeral in 1655, and buried in Henry VII's chapel in Westminster Abbey. At the Restoration his body was thrown out and consigned to a pit, hopefully a midden, behind a prebendal house there.

Sir Thomas Mauleverer was of ancient family and large estates at and around Allerton. A Cambridge man – St John's College – he was one of the oppositionists from Gray's Inn. A daughter married the Regicide Scott. In 1641 Charles I made Mauleverer a baronet in the hope of gaining influential support among the Yorkshire gentry. The attempt was in vain – like so many of Charles's hopeful efforts: he was curiously optimistic. Instead, Mauleverer raised two regiments of foot and a troop of horse for Parliament out of his own pocket. Scott brought before Parliament Mauleverer's petition for £15,000 reimbursement – a clearly exaggerated sum. Parliament granted him £1000 for immediate relief, and ordered the Committee for Northern Affairs to raise the rest, with interest. Such sums were largely extracted from the confiscated estates of Royalists. What a crying waste it all was!

Mauleverer was not a nice man. He was arraigned more than once before Parliament for appropriating horses to his own use, and for vindictive conduct towards neighbours. Naturally he sided with the Army, and attended every session of the High Court. He died in 1655.

However, his son and heir had fought on the Royalist side. This not infrequently happened – useful reinsurance. So the son was allowed to succeed to the baronetcy and a portion of the family estates.

Peregrine Pelham was a Hull man, very influential in the town, especially after marrying Jacoba Van Lore, widow of a wealthy money-lender. Thus sheriff – alderman – mayor. Hull was of great strategic importance, and in Parliament Pelham was much to the fore in naval affairs. A strong Puritan, even 'a fiery spirit', he was a follower of Cromwell and opposed negotiations with the King after the Second Civil War. He accepted appointment to the High Court with enthusiasm, but died next year, still under fifty. Perhaps his fiery spirit wore him out.

Leicestershire produced three renegades, Smith, Temple and Waite. At Oxford **Henry Smith** matriculated from Magdalen Hall (now Hertford), but graduated from St Mary Hall, now part of Oriel.

This was followed by a spell at Lincoln's Inn, from which he joined up with alacrity, like other young sparks. For Leicestershire Smith sat in Parliament with Lord Grey of Groby. Smith's wife was the daughter of Cornelius Holland, another Regicide. One sees how these miscreants pulled together and spoke up for each other. Young Smith followed Holland's lead in the Rump, and voted with Henry Marten.

At his own trial he pleaded his youth in the High Court proceedings, and also 'bad influence' – probably true enough. Committed to the Tower, it seems that he was released before death. Perhaps he was already ill, for he was still in his forties when he died in 1668.

Peter Temple of Sibbesdon was apprenticed when a youth as a linen draper, but succeeded to the family estate on the deaths of his brothers. As High Sheriff of Leicestershire he did good work in Parliament's eyes by repressing the local Baptists. For his services altogether he was awarded £1500 from the confiscations in his county.

Sentenced to be hanged for his part in the High Court, where he had been active, he successfully pleaded the benefit of the Proclamation allowing consideration upon surrender. So he languished for three years in the Tower, where he died of dropsy.

Thomas Waite was another Gray's Inn runagate, who took up arms for Parliament at once, and became a captain under Lord Grey. It was not long before he was involved in a dispute with him, apparently over the Duke of Buckingham's Burley

House in Rutland, of which Waite as governor took a lease. In 1647 he was given an order for over £2000 for expenses he had incurred; by 1650 he had received only £1600. So he was allowed to purchase the Duke's lands he had under lease, at a reduced rate, in lieu of cash.

In the High Court proceedings he was rather remiss, and attended only three sessions. At his own trial he pleaded that he was forced by Cromwell and Ireton to become one of the judges. So he got off the death sentence and was confined in Jersey, where he had the joy of his fellow Regicide Millington's company.

John Moore was a Liverpool man (pronounced in those days Lerpool). Of a well-to-do merchant and shipping family, he was useful in Parliament on committees looking into these affairs. Parliament also sent him back to Lancashire to disarm Recusant Catholics, of whom there were too many. He put up a good fight defending Liverpool against Prince Rupert's attack, who took it. When it was recaptured Moore was made governor. In London he acted as a kind of police officer for Parliament, searching out delinquents' and malefactors' arms. Liverpool was a base for Parliament's campaigns in Ireland, where Moore had a fighting record, though half of his regiment were lost by shipwreck.

After the King's 'trial', at which Moore attended almost every session, he was again used as a police officer to investigate those 'designing any evil' against the Court's members. We may regard this as an indication of its unpopularity. No less symptomatic is the membership of his Committee of the Army, which he ran, every member of which was a Regicide – Ludlow, Scott, Venn, Purefoy.

Moore was evidently found a useful man-of-all-work, and spent his resources doing it. In Ireland again ill of the disease that carried off so many people there – fever, dysentery, malaria, Ireton died there, Cromwell nearly did – Moore died in 1650, the year after his lamentable attendance on what he thought duty in London. He had sacrificed estate and bankrupted himself for the Good Old Cause. Was this altogether wise? Not at all profitable to him, as to some others.

Not far away Shrewsbury was a strong-point for action against Wales. Here **Humphry Edwards**, another Gray's Inn man, had family influence. In January 1642 he had accompanied the King in his disastrous attempt to catch the Five Members, his leading opponents in Parliament. One can't help wishing he had caught them, but the plan was betrayed to Pym by that treacherous intriguer, Lady Carlisle, the unwise Queen's *confidante*.

Edwards, seeing how things were going, then switched sides. He eventually sided with the Radical Army party, voting against any further negotiations with the King and attending his trial. It is nice to think that the Army gave him the job of pursuing the odious Prynne, for publishing his *Brief Memento* – very far from brief, as usual – attacking them, as formerly he had attacked the Queen.

Edwards was one of those who used his position for personal gain. As commissioner in South Wales he made profitable purchases of Church property. More comically, his enemies accused him of incest with his aunt!

Did he die – of it – in 1658? At the Restoration what had stuck to his fingers was confiscated.

George Fleetwood was a kinsman of the too active Army man, General Charles Fleetwood. When only twenty, avid for action, George raised a troop of horse to keep the Chilterns as a defensive barrier for London. When a London mob invaded the Commons in 1647 bent on restoring the King, George took refuge with the Army and shared in their desperate undertakings.

He served as Visitor to purge the university of Oxford and also as Ejector of Anglican clergy. Otherwise he seems to have shared, in the Council of State, 'the moderate majority's reaction against the religious extremists, and in favour of the gentlemen of broad acres' – of which he possessed not a few. Thus Cromwell knighted him, then made him a member of his House of Lords. Reaction was setting in.

In May 1660 George Fleetwood actually supported the mayor at York in proclaiming Charles II. When tried as a Regicide this helped to get him off, along with a tearful submission. His life was spared. Imprisoned in the Tower until 1664, he was then transported to Tangier, a convenient receptacle, where he died in 1672.

Though Norfolk was largely Parliamentarian, and horribly Puritan, **William Hevingham** was its only Regicide. Of ancient stock, and of Pembroke College, Cambridge, his mother was one of the Royalist Pastons. Though he attended the High Court regularly, he did not sign the death warrant. He took the grand opportunity of purchasing confiscated lands of Church, Crown and cavaliers; and speculated heavily in debentures. His various manors brought him in £1000 a year.

At the Restoration he petitioned for mercy, claimed that he had tried to prevent the King's execution, opposed Cromwell's tyranny, and since 1649 had been really a Royalist. True, in 1659 he had contributed to Sir George Booth's premature Rising. With this, and his wife's intercessions, his life was spared; but he remained a prisoner at Windsor Castle until his death in 1678.

His body was given burial in the family church at Ketteringham – no memorial there to the family disgrace.

William Purefoy was most active in his county, Warwickshire. After Cambridge and Gray's Inn he travelled to Geneva, which had an unfortunate effect on his religious and political formation. He became a pure Presbyterian. In Warwickshire he enjoyed the support of the nasty Lord Brooke, who hoped to live to see the day when there would not be one stone upon another left on St Paul's. (He was shot in the eye when aiming at Lichfield cathedral under siege.)

Purefoy was a stern opponent of late negotiations with the King. However, socially conservative, he opposed the abolition of the House of Lords, and was a sound enemy of the Levellers. He believed in a national church, which should be Presbyterian to discipline the people and keep order in the nursery.

A very old man, he died in 1659, when his

attainted goods came to the Crown.

Plymouth was of the utmost strategic importance to Parliament in the West, and remained a thorn in the side of the Royalists in Devon and Cornwall throughout the war. Besieged and threatened by armies it never surrendered.

A successful merchant and Adventurer for Ireland, **Gregory Clement** boasted that he could subdue it with a dozen ships, six pinnaces and sufficient horse and foot. An extremist, he dissented from negotiations with the King, and was regular in attendance at his trial. Shortly after he blotted his own copybook, and was suspended from sitting in the Commons for 'carriage offensive and scandalous to Parliament'. He had been discovered in bed with a maidservant. His name was expunged from that sacred document, the death warrant.

At the Restoration he went into hiding (like Milton), but was discovered – again! – concealed in a house near Gray's Inn. Though he pleaded for mercy, there was no one to speak up for him, and he was executed.

CHAPTER 9

Soldiers and Others

Some Regicides were pure – or, should we say, mere – soldiers. But the Revolution involved them in politics, especially when the Army came to dominate the scene. This was noteworthy in the case of Colonel Pride, for it was Pride's Purge that opened the way for the Army's drastic resolution of affairs – if it lasted only as long as Cromwell lasted.

Thomas Pride was said to have been in his youth a brewer's drayman. The Army gave him his chance, and he did an outstanding job commanding his regiment at Naseby, Bridgwater and Bristol. In the tug-of-war between Army and Parliament, he spoke up for his soldiers' demands. He fought under Cromwell in South Wales, and then went North to trap the mismanaged Scots at Preston. He presented his regiment's petition to the Army Council for punishment of the King, and for the removal from office of the 'contrary-minded'. No opposition was the watch-word.

Pride's Purge followed. It is at least amusing to think of the vociferous Prynne – who had driven Archbishop Laud to his death – having to be pushed, gesticulating and still vociferating – out of the Commons. In the summer of the *annus horribilis* 1649 Pride presented to what he had left of the Rump – over 100 MPs had been ignominiously pushed out – a petition calling for an end to the imposition of Presbyterian conformity, the Solemn Covenant and the rest of it. This was the Army's point of view, for it was the breeding-ground of sects, like insects.

At the battle of Dunbar he commanded a brigade, when the Scots gave their impregnable position away at the behest of their fatuous ministers. Pride was rewarded with a grant of Scottish lands to the tune of £500 a year. Henceforward he was a rich man, knighted by the Lord Protector and promoted to his Upper House. Not bad for a brewer's drayman! He was able to purchase Henry VIII's fantasy palace of Nonsuch which, at the Restoration, was returned to the Crown.

Charles II gave it to the rapacious and insatiable Lady Castlemaine, who proceeded to demolish it and sell the remains. Nothing left of it there today, though a few fragments are to be seen in Surrey country houses.

Pride had died before his come-uppance caught up with him, and was buried at royal Nonsuch. His body was ordered to be exhumed and defiled, since it was defiling the place.

Sir Hardress Waller had been knighted by Charles I at the beginning of his reign, but took to the field against him in the Civil War. For Waller was one of the Protestant landowners in Ireland ruined by the Rising of 1641. And all Protestants thought that

Charles I was soft on Irish Catholics. Naturally enough he wanted to include all the peoples of his three kingdoms in his favour and consideration. The hope proved impossible.

Waller took refuge in the sea-stronghold of Cork, of which he became governor, and from which he advanced into the fighting in Munster. At the formation of the New Model Army he got an English command, and fought at Naseby. In the Second Civil War he was employed in subduing insurrection in Royalist Cornwall, and an attempted recovery of Pendennis Castle. The country at large could never be happy under the rule of the Army. It lay under conquest – the Puritan blight – England no less than Scotland and Ireland.

An Army man, Waller joined its march on London in December 1648 and was a chief associate of Pride in the Purge of Parliament. At the King's 'Trial' he attended every session but one, and took part in the arrangements for his execution.

At the Restoration he first fled to France, then decided to surrender to Charles II's Proclamation. This afforded some hope. Though condemned, he was not executed. He spent some time in the Tower, and then was sent to join the choice company in Jersey. One wonders whether they were allowed to cheer themselves up with an occasional game of bowls?

Isaac Ewer, an Essex man, married an Essex girl, sister of Thurloe, the Protector's Secretary of State. Early on Ewer became captain of a troop of horse, then had a full career in the New Model Army. In the Second Civil War he signalised himself by recovering Chepstow Castle, which had been seized by the Royalists.

He became active in politics through his member-ship of the Council of Army officers, the leading members of which were all Regicides: Ireton, Whalley, Constable, Scrope – with Cromwell in the background. These were the people who drove on the King's 'Trial' and execution. One sees what a purely Army affair it was. Drafted to Ireland, Ewer at once made his will, and thereupon died – as so many did – of the prevalent diseases. Thurloe became the guardian of his children.

Thomas Horton was originally a servant, a falconer to the intriguer Hazelrig, who got Auckland Castle out of the bishopric of Durham. No wonder he was such an upright Puritan! Horton for his part got the lands of the Royalist Langhorne.

Accompanying Cromwell to Ireland, he died within a year of his attentive actions as a Regicide. He left to 'the Major-General my horse called "Haselrig" '. We can hardly suppose that Cromwell liked the name – let us hope that he changed it.

Francis Hacker was a Nottinghamshire man, the only renegade in a Royalist family – one brother was killed fighting for the King, another lost a hand. During the 'Trial' Hacker had personal charge of the King, escorted him with a guard to and from Westminster Hall, was in control of access to him, supervised his execution and signed the baleful order to the executioner.

Hacker campaigned under Cromwell in Scotland, where his regiment served under Major-General

Deane. We find him petitioning with those other familiar figures, Whalley, Goff, Barkstead and Okey. A strict Presbyterian, he discouraged preaching in the ranks – for which Cromwell reproved him – and purged Quakers from his regiment. An adherent of Presbyterian discipline he purged political sectaries too.

On duty as a soldier, he did not sit in the High Court, but for the part he had played he was classed and tried as a Regicide. He pleaded the superior orders under which he had acted, and produced the actual warrant he had been given. He was condemned to be executed nevertheless – it seems a trifle unfair. He could not say much for himself; 'God hath not given me the gift of utterance.' We may well think God had given too many too much. His chief regret was that he had been a persecutor of 'the good people of God who differed from him in judgment'.

His trial on 15 October 1669 throws a lurid light on the last day of Charles I. Hacker had received his warrant in a room at St James's Palace then called the Horn Chamber, while the King lay in the inner room. A witness did not charge Hacker with taking tobacco to the King's offence, 'but the soldiers would be stepping by and taking tobacco at his chamber in St James's, and committed other incivilities'. Some people kept their hats on before him, though the officer giving evidence said, 'I always checked them for it.' The King recognised his consideration. 'That very night before his death he was pleased to give me a legacy, which was a gold toothpicker and case, that he kept in his pocket.'

'The next day, when the warrant came, the guard of halberdiers went with him through St James's

Park, I was present walking near the King, the Bishop of London (now of Canterbury)[1] was with him and some others. As we were going through the Park he was pleased to discourse something touching his burial. He wished that the Duke of Richmond [his Stuart cousin] and some others that he should bring should take care of it. He told me he had some thoughts that his Son might come to bury him, and desired he might not suddenly be buried.'

'When he came to Whitehall he went into a room in the Gallery, the guard stood in the outer room there.' There Mr Henry Seymour brought a letter from the Prince – Hacker allowed him to deliver it and the King read it.

Next Colonel Hercules Hunks (what a name!) who was an assistant that ghastly day, gave his evidence. Early on the day the King died, 'I was in Ireton's chamber, where Ireton and Harrison were in bed together. [Perhaps today one needs to explain that sharing beds was quite regular at that time – and this case was convenient for secret conference.] There was Cromwell, Colonel Hacker, Lt.-Col. Phaire and myself standing at the door.'

Cromwell ordered Hunks to draw up the order for the executioner. Everything was to be in order. Hunks refused to write it, and there ensued some 'cross-passages'. 'Cromwell would have no delay. There was a little table that stood by the door, and pen, ink, and paper being there, Cromwell stepped and writ.' He then handed the paper to Hacker, who subscribed his name, Cromwell berating Hunks for a 'forward peevish fellow'.

---

[1] This was good Bishop Juxon.

Hacker was in command at the scaffold. Another gave evidence that 'coming near the scaffold, as soon as I was engaged in the throng, I could not pass backward nor forward, I was enforced to stand there. During that time I saw the Scaffold and the Axe, and the Block taken up by divers people … His Majesty came to the side of the Scaffold next St James's. He looked that way, and smiled.'

The King found the block too low. The executioner tried the edge of the Axe with his thumb. The King said, 'Hurt not the Axe.' His head was severed at one stroke. When the head was held up bleeding there arose such a groan from the throng as he hoped never to hear again.

Hacker had nothing to say for himself, and made no plea. He merely said briefly that what he had done was by command. To this his Judge said, 'You must understand that no power on earth could authorise such a thing. No command in such a case can excuse you.'

A concession was made to the Royalist family: the body was not quartered but allowed to be buried in their church in the City. And later Hacker's estate was purchased back from the Duke of York by the brother who had lost his hand.

Daniel Axtell – such an ominous name – had been in command of the soldiers in Westminster Hall. A lower-class man – he had begun as a grocer's apprentice – his manners were in accordance. When the masked Lady Fairfax had shouted out that her husband would never be there and Oliver Cromwell was a traitor, Axtell had called out, 'Shoot the drab.'

In Ireland he fought hard, his regiment suffering

heavy losses at Drogheda. A Baptist, he had the bright idea of sponsoring Baptist missionaries to convert the Irish. He had a name for cruelty, and once was suspended for not giving the quarter promised to prisoners. His defence was that God's use for him was to suppress the Irish, and that his heart often fed upon the words of the Bible, 'Give her blood to drink, for she is worthy.' It shows up the deleterious influence the Bible had on Puritans, sanctifying their savagery.

At his trial he spoke up for himself as no one else, making speeches again and again, on or off the point. We learn, but not from him, that when the King 'came by the soldiers that stood with Col. Axtell, his Majesty bowed, and afterwards took off his hat, and went up to the court'.

Axtell proceeded to make some awkward personal points, if nothing to the point of law. 'I am no more guilty than the Lord General Monk, who acted by the same authority.' And then, 'whoever did make any breach upon the House of Commons, they were grandees, persons of a greater quality. I was an inferior officer ... I did nothing but what I was commanded upon pain of death. I was there by a special order, and not by a voluntary act of my own. And so it cannot be, *Compassing the death of* the King', the statutory words of the charge.

He then made a shrewd hit. If he was held guilty of Treason, what about the House of Commons that ordered it? 'Then doubtless they must begin the Treason.' Lawyer Annesley answered, as he had done with others before: 'Who were they? Those few only that remained – almost all the cities, counties and boroughs of England had none left to represent them: they were driven away by force.'

Here was the whole case against the Army: it was totally unrepresentative of England, let alone Scotland and Ireland. Only the King could represent all three. And it was upon this basis – King and full Parliament – that the Restoration rested.

Sir Purback Temple gave evidence as to Axtell's conduct in Westminster Hall: 'I saw him the most activest person there. During the time that the King was urging to be heard, he was then laughing, entertaining his soldiers, scoffing aloud. Whilst some of the soldiers by his suffering did fire powder in the palms of their hands that they did not only offend his Majesty's smell, but enforced him to rise up out of his chair and with his hand to turn away the smoke. After this he turned about to the people and smiled upon them and those soldiers that so rudely treated him.' How vilely the place must have smelt! – and one remembers that Charles I was a fastidious aesthete.

Axtell insisted, 'I was no lawyer, no statesman, no councillor, but a soldier.' So he asked by what authority the charge of treason was justified. He was answered, by the Statute of 25 Edward III. (We remember that it was by this statute still that Roger Casement and William Joyce were condemned in our time.)

There was no hope for Axtell. He suffered the full penalties of the law, declaring that he was dying for the Good Old Cause.

Vincent Potter was something of an exception, for he had emigrated to New England, where he was employed as a soldier, then came back to take a hand in the fray here. He was captain of horse in his native Warwickshire militia, then succeeded his brother, who was slain at Naseby, as Army commissioner. As such he helped to provision Cromwell's campaigns in Scotland and Ireland.

He sat in the High Court and signed the death warrant. For good (or bad) measure he next took part in the group-trial with which the bloodthirsty Army followed up that of the King. His cousin and friend the Duke of Hamilton, who had advised him ill about Scottish affairs; Lord Holland, who had been an opponent then changed sides; Lords Capel and Goring, all were condemned to death. Does one diagnose a class-element here again?

Potter in turn was condemned to death, but his sentence was never carried out – he disappears in prison. He is signalised as 'the only New England Regicide', but need we give New England – whose Puritanism was already sufficiently discreditable – this discredit?

Hugh Peters might be brought under the same heading, since he spent fourteen years in New England. It was the best part of his life, for there he did constructive work, encouraging trade and fisheries, and helping to found Harvard College. He was born at Fowey in Cornwall, of a family of émigré Dutch extraction on one side, and of an ancient Cornish family, the Treffrys, on the other. After Cambridge, a religious malcontent, he went back to Calvinist Holland, which did him no good.

I have hitherto done my best to do him justice,[2] so

---

[2] See my *Four Caroline Portraits*, ch. 4.

here we may concentrate on the part he played in bringing the King to book. As a cleric he was not called to the High Court, so technically he was not a Regicide. But he had preached it up, hence a lot of witnesses were called to corral him – and some of them gave false witness. He had been the most popular turn as a preacher, now he was the most reviled of men; no one spoke a word for him. So much for popularity with the mob.

With so many witnesses his trial was a long one, and the detailed evidence throws a vivid light on what had happened and on Peters himself. Peters had accompanied Cromwell to Ireland, where he caught the prevalent dysentery, he thought by infection from praying over Captain Horton. Returning to Milford Haven he was taken care of by a Dr Young for ten weeks. Young won his confidence, and now betrayed it. Peters had spent a good deal of his own money on the Irish enterprise, and for compensation had received only a small pittance of land from the Marquis of Worcester's estate.

Peters deposed that he had not found a more violent man for the Parliament than Dr Young – he was 'so fierce in that way that his words should be little attended to'. Had he turned round, or was he a spy? For himself, people who knew him realised that in sickness he was liable to be light-headed, hardly responsible for what he said. This was true enough – and not only when sick, but in the pulpit. Another witness as to his words was certain that 'this was the gentleman, for then he wore a great sword'. Peters: 'I never wore a great sword in my life.'

One Starkey deposed that, in the Army proceedings at Windsor – an orgy of prayer and fasting –

Peters was often with Ireton at night. 'Mr Ireton, being civil in carriage, would entertain discourses with Mr Peters', who would say that the King was 'a tyrant, that he was a fool, that he was not fit to be a king'. No doubt that was a view current in the Army, on account of the obstinacy with which he adhered to his opinions. The great Scotch contriver of the Solemn Covenant, Henderson, found the same thing. When he discovered what an able and consistent exposition of his beliefs Charles I could give, it so stunned him that he had a breakdown. He had never conceived that any other views were possible than his own. He was a Presbyterian.

Starkey had seen Peters go up to Ireton's chamber at ten o'clock, and understood that he did not go away till four o'clock in the morning. Ireton seems to have been given to discourse in bed. Another witness had seen Peters riding in triumph like an almoner before the King's coach. 'The King sitting alone in the coach, I did put off my hat, and he was graciously pleased to put off his hat.' To this Peters answered that the King had commanded him to ride ahead, that Bishop Juxon might come up beside him.

Sir Jeremy Whichcote swore that he had several times been in Mr Peters' company, 'by accident, not by choice', and heard him speak very scurrilously of the King. He spoke with great reverence of the High Court, as resembling the trial at the end of the world by the Saints. He had offered to preach before the King, but 'the poor wretch would not hear me'. It was true that Peters had made the impertinent offer, but the King had politely put it off for another time. Instead, someone else had heard Peters preaching before Cromwell and Bradshaw on the text, 'Bind your kings with chains, and your nobles in fetters of iron.' 'I observed that Oliver Cromwell did laugh at that time you were preaching.' Peters was apt to play the buffoon in the pulpit – it is the only time we hear of Oliver Cromwell actually laughing.

Peters was now so reviled that there was a persistent rumour that he was the masked executioner on the scaffold – ordinary humans will believe anything. He was able to prove that he had been away at home sick all that day. His servant gave evidence that he was ill in his chamber all the morning, 'melancholy sick as he used to be'. We know that he was a manic-depressive. As Cromwell was too.

There was no denying that Peters had often preached against the King, as he had been importuned to do, and many London ministers were in it 'deeper than I'. Now he was repentant of his carriage towards the King: 'it is my great trouble, I beg pardon for my own folly and weakness.' He had thought that God had 'a great controversy with the nation', and he must bear his part. Milton thought the same, and got away with it. 'God hath a regard to the people of England. I look upon this nation as the Cabinet of the world.' Just what Milton thought – to set an example for other people. The French Revolutionaries followed suit, consciously and deliberately.

Hugh Peters had done many good deeds and services to people in his time. He cited two from Royalists. Lady Worcester gave testimony under her own hand: 'I do hereby testify that, in all the sufferings of my husband, Mr Peters was my great friend.' The Earl of Norwich had given him his seal as a keep-sake, 'for saving his life, which I will keep as long as I live'. He had not long to live – nobody would save him.

All kinds of slanders flew round about this character, once so popular. One was to the effect that he was unchaste with womenfolk. To a friend who came to question him about it in prison, he was able to assure him that 'he never knew any woman but his own wife, blessed be the Lord'. In fact he had not been much blessed, for his godly Massachusetts wife turned out insane.

The mob were anxious to see how their one-time favourite would meet his end, and he himself was exercised in mind whether he might not go through his sufferings with courage. Chief Justice Cook had been hanged, cut down and quartered before his eyes. 'The hangman came to him all besmeared with blood and, rubbing his bloody hands together, tauntingly said, "Come, Mr Peters, how do you like this work?" To whom he replied, "I am not, I thank God, terrified at it." ' His convictions bore him up. 'What, flesh! Art thou unwilling to go to God through the fire and jaws of death? This is a good day, He is come that I have long looked for, and I shall be with Him in glory.'

So lucky Ludlow tells us, safe in Switzerland, and adds: 'in the meantime it's the hour of the Saints' patience.'

Poor Peters continued to be reviled after his death. One Sunday in April 1663 Mr Pepys went to the chapel in Whitehall – so 'monstrous full I could not go into my pew, but sat among the choir' – to hear an admirable but severe sermon by a Scotchman, Dr Crichton. 'He ripped up Hugh Peters, calling him the execrable skellum, his preaching and stirring up the maids of the City to bring in their bodkins and thimbles.' – For the (bad) Old Cause.

Most of this Scot's sermon was directed against the Presbyterians. It is noticeable that the sermons of the Anglican bishops made them the chief target – the ridiculous sects that the Civil War had propagated were not to be taken seriously.

Since Peters had been such a popular turn in his heyday, he became a rather macabre folk figure with the people:

> Sing hey-ho, my honey,
> My heart shall never rue,
> Twenty-four traitors now for a penny,
> And into the bargain – Hugh.

Many publications, tracts, libels were circulated about him; a History of his Life and Death was translated into Dutch. Even into the nineteenth century he was still celebrated. In 1851 there appeared – appropriately in Boston, Massachusetts – a *Memoir, a Defence of Hugh Peters*, by the Rev. Joseph B. Felt. More curiously, Disraeli's father wrote a 'Vindication of the Character of Hugh Peters', but this remained in manuscript with his son, for whom such characters had no allure.

CHAPTER 10

Consequences

What more remains to be said?

In the first place, and quite obviously, the execution of Charles I led to a great strengthening of the monarchy, in particular to a veritable cult of the sacrificial figure of Charles himself. For years he had been slandered from Puritan pulpits, libelled and attacked in their all too efficient and lying propaganda. It had never been possible to catch up with it, or with the lies about Archbishop Laud. Both had been reviled as Papists, when the truth should have been obvious to all, that they were both loyal to the Church – the King would never save himself, by sacrificing it.

It is difficult to see that he would have recovered enough respect, let alone prestige, to return to rule, even if the belated Treaty of Newport with Parliament had been allowed by the Army to come into operation.

Now, at one blow in the courtyard at Whitehall on 30 January 1649 all that ground was recovered – and more. Monarchy and Church were given a Royal Martyr, and the cult began at once. The publication of the King's Book, *Eikon Basilike* – the portrait of

161

his last days – was worth a victory on the battlefield. And even more, for the effect was lasting. Nothing that John Milton said – in his Puritan propaganda work, *Eikonoklastes* (and it contained a couple of lies) – had the slightest effect.

At the Restoration – which was a restoration of Church as well as King – the Church naturally cashed in on this. The Prayer Book brought up to date, carried a new service commemorating the Martyr for the 30th of January – and this continued in use for at least the next century. (As boy and youth I observed the date.) Everywhere in loyal Cornwall the King's nobly phrased Letter of Thanks (no doubt written by Clarendon), for the county's loyalty in his campaign of 1644, was posted up in the churches – one can still read it there. Everywhere the Royal Arms went up – in the neighbourhood of the victory at Stamford Hill, splendid specimens of coloured plasterwork by a local master-craftsman.

At Falmouth the new church that was building in 1640 was named Charles Church by Parliament, for silly Puritans would not recognise the existence, or name, of Saints. (They applied that title to themselves.) With the Restoration it became the church of King Charles the Martyr. What ordinary folk felt we have some indication from the neighbouring county, where a Devon fellow came out with 'the King was a God' compared with what followed – though the poor fellow had not the advantage of knowing Frazer's anthropological work, *The Golden Bough*, with its account of the ritual sacrifice of sacred monarchs.

The Restoration was also the restoration of aristocracy and the greater gentry at the centre of affairs in Westminster. Some historians today go so far as to describe it as the victory of the county gentry – after the obvious failure of the Puritan Revolution. That disillusioning experience could not have maintained itself much longer, against the balance of social forces in the country, the 'natural order' of things. Indeed it had held only as long as Cromwell was there to maintain the unity of the Army.

How much longer he could have held the fort is a question. It seems that he died in disillusionment and something like despair. Had it been a mistake, after all the victories, which he had taken as signs from Providence? The cry came from the great man's heart: 'That which you have by force, I look upon it as nothing.' He longed to achieve something like consensus, or just acceptance, from the English people. But this was impossible: the Revolution had been made by force, and Puritan propaganda. With his death the force was dissolving, in 1659 the Army was splitting asunder into different camps, generally hated by the people; while Puritan propaganda was no longer believed – it never had been by the nation at large. It was contrary to the nature of the English people.

Now the governing class, taught by its nasty experience, was coming together. Its Parliamentary half, which had won the Civil War, expelled from power by the revolutionary Purge, was affronted and shocked by the execution of the King. Even the small group of republican doctrinaires, some of whom had become Regicides, had gone into opposition at Cromwell's becoming Lord Protector. Take the case of Colonel Hutchinson, who had won

Nottingham for Parliament. He was in open opposition to Cromwell even before he became Protector. This served as an argument in his favour, and helped – along with the lobbying of his Royalist relations – to get him off at his own trial (unfairly, and to the wounding of his exquisite Puritan conscience).

The governing classes had been foolish to allow their conflict for power, along with their religious preferences and illusions, to go so far as to involve them in civil war. This had been precipitated from fanatic Scotland and murderous Ireland, not from reluctant England. It is the conflict for power that is fundamental, and the approach through class-conflict that illuminates it, enables us to understand it.

In seventeenth-century circumstances it is unthinkable that there could have been *social* revolution. Society could never have been run on the basis of a lot of Levellers and Diggers, Ranters and Fifth Monarchy men, Muggletonians, Soul-sleepers, Anabaptists, Quakers, all quarrelling like mad – for all the absurd respect given them today by their academic descendants. One observes how easily the Levellers were dealt with by the Army's 'whiff of grape-shot' at Burford.

The facts of class are ultimately decisive. The nobility and greater gentry, largely Royalist, had been defeated in the war. The Parliamentary cause was backed on the whole by lesser gentry, along with middle and merchant classes. Though the county gentry lost power at the centre, with the Revolution, they retained their power in the parishes, at the foundation of society. All through the brief experience of Revolution one sees what a struggle the revolutionary group at Westminster had to get respectable people to fill offices and carry on administration in the counties. They did their best – Cromwell took particular personal trouble – but could recruit only lesser people to carry on the work. No doubt it was unfair of Royalist gentry to regard it as the rule of 'the butcher, the baker and the candlestick-maker', but that caricature represented a truth.

We should, by the way, refer to the Parliamentary section of the gentry as 'Parliament-men', rather than 'Presbyterians', as is usual. Though they may have been Puritans, they did not stand for the beauty of full-blown Presbyterianism.

With the Restoration the upper classes returned not only 'in force' at the centre, but got their revenge in their localities. Plymouth provides a prime example. The townsmen had remained faithful to Parliament and Puritanism throughout the horrid period, war and revolution, 1642-1660. Now the West Country gentry got their revenge: they simply sacked most of the corporation. Not only that, they built a massive citadel which looks not so much out to sea, but frowns down upon the Barbican and the huddled townsmen below. Upon the grand baroque gateway are not only the Royal Arms but those of the Earl of Bath. This was that John Grenville who, as a boy, had been lifted on his father's horse, when Sir Bevil was killed at Lansdown.

What the gentry *felt* about their experience of revolution may be seen by what one of these same Devon gentry wrote about the Cromwellian customs official, one Hatsell, who – so far as is known – was a decent fellow. The gent, however, writing to his brother-in-law, says, 'I suppose your friend Hatsell, that threatened to make you stink, smells ugly himself now.' I do not know if they managed to throw him out. In aristocratic circumstances, patronage became the order of the day, and one observed them forking in their dependents. 'Godliness' ceased to be a prime qualification. One already sees the social tradition of English upper-class families coming forward: eldest son to succeed to the inheritance, second son for Army or Navy, youngest for the Church, often a family living reserved for him.

The restoration of the Church was a more ticklish and complex business, for the Parliament men who, in alliance with the Royalists, had brought Charles II back were still, though not pure Presbyterians, infected, we may say, with Puritanism. However, the clerical hierarchy was at once restored, bishops, deans and chapters, parochial clergy, in parallel with nobles, gentry, people.

The young King and Clarendon were politic and moderate, they wished for comprehension and to include as many of the reasonable Puritan clergy as possible. Their leading figures, Richard Baxter and several others were offered bishoprics. Baxter, who could not agree with anybody, or even with himself for long – everybody else was out of step but he – refused. Cromwell's brother-in-law, the sensible and scientific Wilkins, accepted. He had told the Protector that religion in England could not be run without bishops. Then he became bishop of Chester, to set a neighbourly model of toleration there – as the unreasonable Baxter could have done at

Hereford when invited.

The aged Bishop Juxon became archbishop. He had been on the scaffold with Charles I, to receive his last injunction, 'Remember!', and had accompanied the corpse weeping to the sad and silent burial at Windsor on a snowy day – the Prayer Book service forbidden. Now the Prayer Book came back with a rush – even the Protector's daughter had been married by it. Little Mr Pepys noticed how quickly in the metropolis, so lately a hot-bed[1] of Puritanism, Laud's precept of bowing to the altar and at the name of Jesus was in evidence. Shortly altars, communion rails, fonts were restored. – As one goes about the country today one notices how many fonts date back to the Restoration.

It may be imagined that all this was not to the fancy of the old Puritans. The aged Juxon was succeeded as archbishop by a veritable statesman, Gilbert Sheldon, who had kept hold of the strings and contacts of the Church all through the disagreeable Puritan *épopée*. His was a masterly performance, a born organiser and administrator. It was remarkable that he, like Clarendon, all through those discouraging years, had never given up hope of the country's eventual return to sanity. It seems that they both had a surprising confidence in the character of the English people, and that things would right themselves.

Sheldon had been turned out of the Warden's Lodgings at All Souls, to be accompanied by the sympathies of the crowd in the High Street. (Most of the Heads of Houses at Oxford and Cambridge were

[1] A dictionary definition of 'hot-bed' is 'a mass of decaying vegetable matter'.

extruded by the Revolution.) Now Sheldon was to address himself to the task of recovery and reconstruction with tireless industry. It does not appear that he regretted the failure of 'comprehension', to include factious Puritan clergy in the renewed Church. From his experience in the country he knew too well their character, and was probably relieved to see their backs. On St Bartholomew's Day 1662, some 1200 of them refused to take the oaths of submission and went out to tread the dreary corridors of Dissent.

From Laud's disheartening experience one may reflect that it was probably easier to deal with the fractious outside the Church than within it. Sheldon had more than enough to cope with in these years. When he gave the magnificent Sheldonian Theatre to Oxford, he was too hard at work even to come down to his old university for its opening. It was the first architectural work of the All Souls man, Wren, nephew of the Laudian Bishop Wren, who had remained in the Tower all through these evil years, refusing Cromwell's blandishments to come out. The great man's heart ached for acceptance, but few respectable people – Parliament men or Royalists – would accept the Revolution.

As for the Regicides, their name was held in horror. Take the case of the Fifth Monarchy man, John Carew. As a rare example of a gentleman of ancient family, the Carews of Antony in Cornwall, he was their leading figure (Harrison had been but a butcher in origin). After Carew's hanging and the rest of it, Charles II conceded his corpse to the family for burial. But I cannot find where, or any particulars of his private life. Enough is known about his public activity during the Revolution, but one cannot find where his property was, where he lived in the country, or whether he married and had children. The family must have closed down on his disgrace – and no wonder. Apart from his religious mania he seems to have been a practical man of business, active on the Rump's committees for maritime and commercial affairs.

The lands of the bishops and of deans and chapters were restored, like those of the Crown. It has been observed that the revolutionary groups made their best profits out of Crown properties. However, it is nice to think of the horrid Hazelrig, though he had been too spry to be a Regicide, having to hand back Auckland Castle to the bishop of Durham. In that diocese the Laudian Bishop Cosin did a grand work of restoration, in the cathedral, at Durham and Auckland Castles, and in the parish churches – as well as founding hospitals and almshouses. Everywhere one goes in his county one notices the rich Restoration woodwork – the medieval woodwork of the cathedral had all been burnt as firewood by the Scotch troops. At Carlisle cathedral the medieval nave the barbarians wrecked was never restored.

An enormous amount of restoration, reconstruction, rebuilding was undertaken throughout the country to recover some of the devastation and sheer destruction of the Puritan period. Especially for the Church – cathedrals, churches and their equipment, bishops' palaces, cathedral closes, housing for the parish clergy. We have noticed the Puritan hatred of the cathedrals, altars, fonts, organs and the divine music of their services. The fanatic Lord Brooke (of

Saybrooke, Mass.) hoped, as we saw, to 'live to see not one stone of St Paul's left upon another'. He was happily killed in helping to destroy Lichfield cathedral – which had largely to be rebuilt, along with the bishop's palace and much of the Close.

Similar work went on all over the country – though nothing could bring back the wonders of medieval stained glass deliberately destroyed, brasses ripped up, sculpture ruined, books, pictures, manuscripts, music burned, silver and plate sold off. Puritan damage to interiors needed to be reformed. At Exeter, where the cloister was turned into a wool-market and then pulled down, the nave was divided in two by a brick wall, for the benefit of Presbyterian and Independent congregations to compete with each other's cacophony.

Many medieval buildings were damaged or lost beyond repair. Still, repairs went forward, other buildings replaced (e.g. the bishop's pretty palace at Winchester), with energy and dedication all over the country. Everywhere church equipment needed replacement – the whole magnificent silver with which Charles I furnished St George's chapel, Windsor, for example – chalices, communion cups, flagons, patens, etc. If one has any sense for local history, one can see the evidences in practically every parish. It makes a subject worth study in itself, for any historian with aesthetic sense – and much more rewarding than studying the varieties of 'thinking' the sects indulged in.

The secular field of study is no less wide, and of great architectural interest. Many medieval castles of the nobility had been ordered to be 'slighted' – i.e. half-ruined, their keeps rendered indefensible. Here

the factor of class configuration, the motive of class
envy, becomes visible to anyone with an appre-
ciative eye. Some among the nobility – though
returned to political power and influence – did not
return to their ruined, ravaged residences. At
Basing there was little left for the Marquis of
Winchester to return to. The Beaufort family did not
return to beautiful Raglan, but built themselves a
new palace at Badminton. Hardly anything was left
of Montgomery Castle – and one sees evidences of
wreck in the church (as indeed at Basing);
henceforth these Herberts concentrated on Powis.

All this encouraged work, industry and
craftsmanship of every kind. It has been noticed how
quickly the country recovered economically – though
aesthetic losses can never be replaced. There was
plenty of work to be done – and working people kept
at their proper jobs doing it. The Restoration gentry
did not encourage ignorant and ill-equipped
tradesmen pursuing mental will-o'-the-wisps. They
disciplined them – and the country prospered.

Not that Restoration society was to everyone's
taste. It amuses one to come across in a country
church in Middlesex, the opinion of a London
Ironmonger, son of a Caroline Lord Mayor,
deploring upon his monument of 1685 'this corrupt,
seditious and wicked age'. He must have been a
crusty 'Country' Tory.

Restored Church lands made a fine field for
investment by the county gentry recovering breath –
beneficial leases to be made by their relations and
friends on the episcopal bench or in cathedral and
collegiate chapters. In taxation they were privileged:

the grander gentry of £1000 or £1200 a year paid no more than the lesser gentry of £250 or £300. In the counties they resumed their place as JPs and at quarter sessions, the real rulers of the county. During the Interregnum government had great difficulty in filling up these places – and had to descend to noticeably lower social levels.

Most important, the gentry were determined to hold on to their control of the civilian militia. No standing Army! – even though this created difficulty for government in waging war abroad. Returned in triumph to Westminster, the gentry in Parliament kept a tight hand on finance. Charles II's government was not allotted enough for all-government purposes – hence his resort to Louis XIV for subsidies.

As for the Puritan morality campaign, a fine example was now set by the restored Court of Charles II! Charles I's Court had been altogether more refined and exemplary, as even supercilious Mrs Hutchinson allowed. Now the Monarch of Great Britain, Grammont commented, was the most conspicuous enemy of female chastity in the country. Charles said peaceably that he never thought a man would be consigned to perdition for going a little out of the way in that regard. His brother James followed suit – except that he took his mistresses for penances, according to Charles. It must be allowed that his women were unscrupulous gold-diggers (their example followed in our time by the grasping Mrs Simpson).

On the other hand, the Purity campaign of the Puritans always was nonsense. The Adultery Act of 1650, which made adultery punishable by death, was so shocking as to be inoperative – contrary to sense and to human nature, like so much of their vaticinations. Still, all through the 1650s they carried on their campaign against fornication. Each year the statistics increased. It would be improper to conclude that there was *more* fornication under their heavenly dispensation, merely that more people were sued. It was one of the objectives of Cromwell's experiment in appointing Major-Generals to oversee people's doings, in the twelve districts into which the country was divided up for the purpose – it lasted for only eighteen months in 1655-6.

See how it worked! In 1665 in Devon, which was part of the area under Major-General Desborough, another cousin of Cromwell's, 20 persons were imprisoned for fornication, of whom 19 were women. We see how unfairly this worked out for women – men mostly denied the offence; anyhow consequences were apt to be less visible. It gives some confirmation to the Puritan bias against women, to which their great poet gave immortal expression. (No such bias in William Shakespeare! We may regard Milton as the great poet of non-conformity, as Shakespeare was of conformity.)

Now, 'the Restoration of King Charles II' observes the historian of the period, Sir George Clark, 'released the English people from the fears and repressions of nearly twenty years. All over the country the maypoles were set up again [with their Freudian significance, appreciated by Puritans], loyal toasts were drunk immoderately. Puritanism was repudiated and derided.' Good times had come again, if not for all. Even the Whig Trevelyan allows that the Restoration was 'the salvation of the country'.

The merry-go-round was led by Charles II. He never lost his popularity whatever he did – and some of what he did was contrary to the country's interests – such was the attachment to monarchy which the martyrdom of his father had won. Even when the religious foolery of James II threw everything of his away, the governing class was careful to retain monarchy in the Revolution of 1688–9. That event did not merit the name of 'revolution': it was merely a change of an inept monarch for his able son-in-law. Everybody knew that James was a fool. His clever brother Charles: 'Nobody is going to kill me, Jamie, to make you king'; and he gave James three years in which to cook his goose – which turned out about right. We may take the evidence of three clever women as to his stupidity. Sarah Churchill observed him over a long period from close at hand. Catherine Sedley observed blithely that she was too plain for a mistress, 'and if I have got wit [i.e. intelligence] he hasn't got enough to know that I have any'. When he turned up in France for well-deserved exile, Mme de Sévigné was astonished to hear him talk about his troubles as if they were those of somebody else, and he had no part in them. The monarchy survived even him.

We must not be so unfair as to deprive the Restoration of its discredit (or credit) as Reaction. Socially and educationally it may fairly be regarded as retrogressive. Hardly any more schools were founded, when, earlier in the century, before the Civil War, had been a great time for the founding of schools. Large areas of the country went without educational provision. The universities declined, except as clerical seminaries for the conformist Church. It was noticeable how quickly Reaction gathered after the first uncertain years of the Restoration. A severe code of repression of dissenters – in other words, Puritans – was brought in by the gentry-dominated, Cavalier Parliament. It was hard luck on Clarendon that it was given his name, the Clarendon Code, for he was not responsible for it and did not favour it. It was the upper classes getting their own back, enforcing order upon people who had made the Revolution.

However, it was on this basis, the reaction from revolution, the social and political structure made solid and safe in 1688–9, that the country made such progress, economically, industrially, politically, at home and abroad, as to be admired as a model on the continent, from France to Russia, from Montesquieu and Voltaire to Catherine the Great.

That governing class, the ablest in Europe, with its naval, commercial and colonial achievements, made Britain a world power.

Today, all whittled away.

Sources

Quotations, unless otherwise specified, are mainly from the following:

The Dictionary of National Biography is of special value for this period, since many of the relevant biographies are by Sir Charles Firth, the leading authority on the seventeenth century.

... Accompt of the Indictment, Arraignment, Trial ... of Twenty Nine Regicides ... 1679.

The Memoirs of Edmund Ludlow., ed. C.H. Firth, 2 vols.

Edmund Ludlow, *A Voyce from the Watch Tower*, ed. A.B. Worden, Camden Soc., 1978.

Aubrey's *Brief Lives*, ed. Andrew Clark, 2 vols., 1898.

The Diary of Samuel Pepys, ed. H.B. Wheatley, 3 vols.

Biographical Dictionary of British Radicals in the 17th century, ed. R.L. Greaves and R. Zaller, 3 vols.

C.V. Wedgwood, *A Coffin for King Charles: The Trial and Execution of Charles II*.

Charles Firth, *Oliver Cromwell and the Rule of the Puritans in England*.

G.N. Clark, *The Later Stuarts, 1660–1714*, Oxford History of England.

G.N. Clark, *English History: A Survey*.
G.M. Trevelyan, *History of England*.

Many county histories, for example:

A.C. Wood, *Nottinghamshire in the Civil War*.
A. Fletcher, *A County Community in Peace and War: Sussex 1600–1660*.
S.K. Roberts, *Recovery and Restoration ... Devon Local Administration, 1646–1670*.
M. Coate, *Cornwall in the Great Civil War and Interregnum, 1642–1660*.

Index

Index

Index

Index